hands-On BiBLE curriculum™

Grades 3 and 4

Winter

Teacher Guide

JESUS' BIRTH

JESUS' MIRACLES

JESUS, OUR FRIEND

Group

Loveland, Colorado

Group

**Hands-On Bible Curriculum™
Grades 3 and 4
Winter**

Copyright © 1993, 1995, and 1997 Group Publishing, Inc.

Second Printing, 1997 edition

Visit our Web site: **www.grouppublishing.com**

Credits
Contributing Authors: Dennis Castle, Jefferson Root, and Carol Younger
Editors: Jennifer Root Wilger, Lois Keffer, and Jan Kershner
Senior Editors: Lois Keffer and Paul Woods
Chief Creative Officer: Joani Schultz
Copy Editor: Ann Marie Rozum
Art Director: Kathy Benson
Cover Art Director: Janet A. Barker
Cover Designer: Marcie Miller
Designer: Lisa Chandler
Computer Graphic Artist: Joyce Douglas
Cover Photographer: Craig DeMartino
Illustrators: Michael Fleishman, Ron Rodrigo, and Elizabeth Woodworth
Audio Engineer: Steve Saavedra
Production Manager: Alexander Jorgensen

ISBN 0-7644-0160-2
Printed in the United States of America.

CONTENTS

■ ■ ■ ■ ■ ■ ■ ■ ■ ■ ■ ■ ■

HOW TO USE THIS BOOK

■ ■ ■ ■ ■ ■ ■ ■ ■ ■ ■ ■ ■

FREE TEACHING TIPS

To help make your teaching more effective, Group provides teaching tips on the Group Publishing Web site.

To get to this Web site, you'll need your own Internet access plus a World Wide Web browser that supports Java™ script and applets. We recommend the newest version of Microsoft Internet Explorer or Netscape Navigator. You can download these browsers from their Web sites if you do not already have one installed.

Once you have these necessary items, use your browser to connect to Group Publishing's Web site at http://www.grouppublishing.com. Click on the button for Lesson Updates for Hands-On Bible Curriculum service.

WHY HANDS-ON BIBLE CURRICULUM™?

There's nothing more exciting than helping kids develop a relationship with Jesus Christ. But keeping kids interested in Bible study and Christian growth can be a challenge. Many kids complain that Bible lessons are boring—just more of the same old thing.

We've found a way to get kids excited about studying the Bible. Each quarter of Hands-On Bible Curriculum™ is packed with fresh, creative, *active* programming that will capture kids' interest and keep them coming back for more.

Here's why Hands-On Bible Curriculum will work for you.

A NEW APPROACH TO LEARNING

Research shows that kids remember about 90 percent of what they *do*, but less than 10 percent of what they *hear*. What does this say to us? Simply that kids don't learn by being lectured! They need to be actively involved in lively experiences that bring home the lesson's point.

Group's Hands-On Bible Curriculum uses a unique approach to Christian education called active learning. In each session students participate in a variety of fun and memorable learning experiences that help them understand one important point. As each activity unfolds, kids discover and internalize biblical truths. Because they're *doing* instead of just listening, kids remember what they learn.

Each Hands-On Bible Curriculum lesson for third and fourth grade is based on an important Bible story. Each lesson point distills the Bible story into a simple, memorable Bible truth third- and fourth-graders can apply to their lives.

Your students will be fascinated with the neat gadgets and gizmos packed in the Learning Lab®. And you'll feel good about seeing kids grow spiritually while they're having fun. Keep students interested by revealing the gizmos one by one as the lessons unfold. Be sure to collect the gizmos after each activity so they don't distract students during the discussion that follows. Some Learning Lab items may be used in several lessons, so be sure to hang on to them until this Teacher Guide informs you they are no longer needed.

In each lesson you'll find a photocopiable "Hands-On Fun at Home" handout to send home with kids. Besides providing an important link between home and church, "Hands-On Fun at Home" features great cartoons, family activities, and "Check It Out" Scriptures and questions to get kids and parents talking about the point of the lesson. You can encourage parents' involvement during the next 13 weeks by mailing photocopies of the letter to parents found on page 11.

The items listed below are typical supplies that may be used in the lessons in this book. Other items required for teaching are included in the Learning Lab. We recommend that your students use their own Bibles in this course so they can discover for themselves the value and relevance of the Scriptures.

- candles
- cassette player
- chalkboard and chalk
- construction paper
- crayons or markers
- glue or glue sticks
- masking tape
- matches
- name tags
- newsprint

- paper clips
- pencils
- plain paper
- plastic trash bags
- scissors
- snacks
- stapler
- 3x5 cards
- thumbtacks
- transparent tape

SUCCESSFUL TEACHING— YOU CAN DO IT!

What does active learning mean to you as a teacher? It takes a lot of pressure off because the spotlight shifts from you to the students. Instead of being the principal player, you become a guide and facilitator—a choreographer of sorts! These ideas will get you started in your new role.

● **Read over your lesson ahead of time.** Hands-On Bible Curriculum lessons are simple to prepare. If you don't want to be tied to your Teacher Guide, consider copying the discussion questions onto a chalkboard or flip chart. Kids can also refer to these written questions to refresh their memories during small group discussions.

● **Be creative in your use of classroom space.** Move your table aside so kids can move around freely and work in groups. Have chairs available but be willing to sit on the floor as well. Chairs can be a distraction, and moving them around slows down your lesson.

● **Think about open areas in the church.** These might be available for activities—the foyer, the front of the sanctuary, a side yard, or parking lot. Kids love variety; a different setting can bring new life and excitement to your lessons.

● **Get to know the students in your class.** When you meet your students for the first time, call them by name. Find out about their lives away from church. Learn and recognize their strengths. Make affirmation a regular part of your class. Be sure to compliment your students when you see them practicing what they've learned.

● **Be sure to help kids tie each experience to the lesson's point.** The lesson's main point is identified by the pointing finger icon each time it occurs in the text. The Point is worded so kids can easily remember and apply it. Be sure to repeat The Point as it's written each time it appears. You may feel you're being redundant, but you're actually helping kids remember an important Bible truth. Studies show people need to hear new information up to 75 times to learn it. Repetition can be a good thing!

● **Always discuss each activity with your students.** Don't skip over the discussion part of an activity in order to complete additional activities. The activities allow children to *experience* Bible truths. The printed discussion questions and summary statements help students explore their feelings, discover important principles, and decide how to apply these principles to their lives.

● **As you lead discussions with your class, ask open-ended questions.** Rather than rephrasing questions as statements and asking children to agree, wait for kids to answer on their own. Pretend you don't know the answer and let the kids teach you. You'll be surprised how much they know!

● **Encourage kids to explain their answers and learn from each other.** With each discussion question, we've included several possible answers. These answers can help prepare you for responses children might give. You can even use them as prompts if your class has trouble thinking of responses. However, these are not meant to be the "right" answers. Accept any and all answers your kids give.

● **Remember that kids learn in different ways.** Don't shy away from an activity just because you've never done anything like it before. It may be just what's needed to help one of your students get the point.

● **Make your class a "safe zone" for kids with special needs and learning disabilities.** Avoid calling on students to read or pray aloud if they find it embarrassing. Talk to the parents of kids with disabilities to find out how best to help them.

Assure students that *all* believers are part of the body of Christ, each with special talents and gifts they can use to serve him.

● **Know your students.** Refresh your memory on what it was like to be a third- or fourth-grader by scanning the chart on page 10. While not exhaustive, this chart will help you know a bit more about the needs, wants, and abilities of the third- and fourth-graders you'll be spending the next 13 weeks with.

● **Capitalize on your students' strengths.** Learn to let your students shine by drawing on their strengths and allowing each of them to make positive contributions to the class. When you're forming groups, include active students with quiet, thoughtful ones. Try pairing children who know the Bible story with children who are hearing it for the first time. Let your students teach each other.

● **If children know a Bible story well, invite them to help you tell it.** Encourage them to share their knowledge with the class and be ready to fill in if they've forgotten parts of the story.

ATTENTION, PLEASE!

Stand back and get ready for a radical idea: Noise can be a good thing in Sunday school! Educators will tell you that kids process new information best by interacting with one another. Keeping kids quiet and controlled doesn't necessarily mean your class is a success. A more accurate barometer might be happy, involved, excited students moving around the classroom, discussing how to apply to their lives the new truths they're learning.

Third- and fourth-graders move fast. If they finish an activity early, you may hear them talking to their friends about school or home life. Or you may see them wrestling or playing together. If you feel as though your room is full of peripheral chatter and motion, don't worry. Kids are used to noisy environments. They're learning a lot in spite of the commotion.

However, you'll need to listen closely for "bad noise"—putdowns, conflicts, and anger. If kids are tormenting or distracting one another during an activity, call for their attention and explain why the behavior is unacceptable. If you have one or two children who are constantly disruptive, make sure they're not sitting together.

Here are some other tips that will help you keep control.

● **Keep things moving!** Most kids have about a seven-minute attention span—the amount of time between TV commercials. That means you need to be ready to move on to the next activity *before* kids get bored with the current one.

If your kids are too lively to learn during an activity, take a break and use up some energy. Have kids sing an action song, run a relay race, or do some jumping jacks and stretches. Then return to the lesson. You'll find that your students will be able to focus much better. For more ideas, try *Fidget Busters: 101 Quick Attention-Getters for Children's Ministry*, available from Group Publishing, Inc., P.O. Box 485, Loveland, CO 80539.

● **Establish attention-getting signals.** Flashing the lights or raising your hand will let kids know it's time to stop what they're doing and look at you. You'll find a suggestion for a classroom signal in the introduction to each four- or five-week module. Rehearse this signal with your students at the beginning of each class so they'll know how to respond. Once your kids become familiar with the signal, regaining their attention will become an automatic classroom ritual.

● **Participate, don't just observe.** Your enthusiasm will draw kids into an activity and help them see you as a friend, not just someone in authority. Get down to kids' eye level so they don't think of you as just another adult, but as an accessible, caring friend.

● **Look for teachable moments.** An activity that seems to be a flop may provide a wonderful opportunity for learning if you ask questions such as "Why didn't this work out?" "How is this like what happens in real life?" and "What can we learn from this experience?" Sometimes children learn even *more* from an activity you felt was a flop!

● **Make the lessons work for your group.** The Teacher Tips in the margins of each lesson suggest ways to adapt the activities for classes of varying sizes. You can use the Bonus Ideas beginning on page 155 to lengthen the lesson. Or use the ideas found in "Remembering the Bible" in the introduction to each module to help kids learn the module's key verse. These fun, active memory-verse activities will help kids remember and apply God's Word in ways that will really make a difference in their lives.

● **If you have a large group or a short class session, pick three or four of the activities you think will work well with your class.** Because you make The Point during each activity, you'll have taught something significant even if you don't get through the whole lesson.

● **If time is running short, finish the current activity and then skip ahead to the closing.** Although kids focus on The Point in each activity, the closing usually includes a prayer and commitment in addition to The Point. The closing activity will reinforce the lesson's point once more and provide a wrap-up for the entire experience.

● **Use the Time Stuffers.** These independent-learning activities will keep kids occupied (and learning!)

　✓　when they arrive early,
　✓　when an individual or a group finishes an activity before the others, or
　✓　when there is extra time after the lesson.

You'll find a Time Stuffer in the introduction to each module. After a quick setup, kids can use the activity during all the lessons of the four- or five-week module.

● **Rely on the Holy Spirit to help you.** Don't be afraid of kids' questions. Remember, the best answers are those the kids find themselves—not the ones teachers spoon-feed them.

UNDERSTANDING YOUR THIRD- AND FOURTH-GRADERS

PHYSICAL DEVELOPMENT

Most:
- Work quickly and with good fine-motor coordination.
- Want frequent repetition of activities they've enjoyed.
- Are interested in active games and organized activities.

EMOTIONAL DEVELOPMENT

Most:
- Have feelings that may be hurt easily.
- Are sensitive to praise and criticism from adults.
- Are developing the ability to empathize with others.

SOCIAL DEVELOPMENT

Most:
- Want to be part of a group.
- Enjoy extended group projects.
- Are able to accept limited constructive criticism.
- Naturally avoid interaction with the opposite sex.

MENTAL DEVELOPMENT

Most:
- Can read well.
- Like to be challenged but don't like to fail.
- Need to feel independent; don't always want help from teachers.
- Understand cause and effect; like to arrange and organize information.

SPIRITUAL DEVELOPMENT

Most:
- Are able to accept that there are some things about God we don't understand.
- Are ready to relate individual Bible events to the scope of Bible history.
- Recognize the difference between right and wrong; able to make deliberate choices about actions.

Dear Parent,

I'm so glad to be your child's teacher this quarter. With our Hands-On Bible Curriculum™, your child will look at the Bible in a whole new way.

For the next 13 weeks, we'll explore Bible stories and topics to help third- and fourth-graders grasp the importance of Jesus' birth, explore God's miraculous power, and learn how to form lasting friendships. Using active-learning methods and a surprising assortment of gadgets and gizmos (such as "metallic ribbons," "neon loops," and "stacking clowns"), we'll help kids discover meaningful applications of God's Word.

Our Hands-On Bible Curriculum welcomes you to play an important part in what your child learns. **Each week kids will receive "Hands-On Fun at Home" handouts to take home and share.** "Hands-On Fun at Home" is a handout containing great crafts, family activities, and "Check It Out" Scriptures and questions—all focused on the point of our Bible lesson for the week.

Let me encourage you to use the "Hands-On Fun at Home" handout regularly; it's a great tool for reinforcing Bible truths and promoting positive, healthy communication in your family.

Sincerely,

JESUS' BIRTH

■ ■ ■ ■ ■ ■ ■ ■ ■ ■ ■ ■ ■

People love the story of Jesus' birth. Even kids who have never been to Sunday school may know something about Mary and Joseph. Some versions of this well-loved story blend the scriptural accounts with ideas found in television specials, popular Christmas songs, and local Nativity scenes. An innkeeper is never mentioned in the Bible. Neither is a donkey, though we hope that Mary did have something to help her make the 75-mile journey from Nazareth to Bethlehem.

Third- and fourth-graders have heard the Christmas story many times. But with all of the activity and excitement competing for their attention during the Christmas season, they may not grasp the Christmas story's importance. The birth of Jesus marked the beginning of a new relationship between God and people. Use these lessons to help your students realize that Jesus' birth can touch their lives just as it touched the lives of Mary, Joseph, and the shepherds.

JESUS' BIRTH

LESSON	PAGE	THE POINT	THE BIBLE BASIS
1—ANYTHING'S POSSIBLE!	17	All things are possible with God.	Luke 1:5-25, 57-66
2—WHO, ME?	27	God uses ordinary people.	Luke 1:26-45
3—GOD'S SON IS BORN	37	Jesus is God's Son.	Luke 2:1-20
4—WHAT ARE WE WAITING FOR?	49	God rewards those who trust him.	Luke 2:21-38
5—READY, SET, GROW!	59	God wants us to learn and grow.	Luke 2:41-52

THE SIGNAL

During the lessons on Jesus' birth, bring kids together by ringing the *gold foil bell* found in the Learning Lab. In response to this signal, kids should immediately stop talking, raise their hands, and focus on you for their next instructions.

Tell kids about this signal—and practice it—before each lesson begins. Explain that it's important to respond to this signal quickly so the class can do as many fun activities as possible. During the lessons, you'll be prompted when to use the signal.

LEARNING LAB

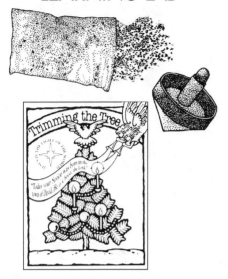

LEARNING LAB

THE TIME STUFFER

This module's Time Stuffer will encourage kids to create cards and ornaments they'll use to share the joy of Christmas with others. Set up a learning center with construction paper, crayons, scissors, glue, and markers for kids to use during their free time. Also include the *top pens* and some of the *sequin dust* found in the Learning Lab. Be sure to show kids how the *top pens* come apart. If you'd like to bring in additional supplies, kids would enjoy craft items such as glitter glue, sequins, and confetti. Hang the Learning Lab's "Trimming the Tree" poster near the learning center.

Post a list of people or groups who might like to receive a Christmas card from your class. Encourage kids to add to the list. When students have free time during the lessons, they can make Christmas cards for the people on the list. Collect any unfinished cards at the end of each class session and bring them back for kids to work on the following week. Attach a "clothesline" of yarn or string on the wall near the learning center to display the cards. Have kids clip their cards to the string or hang them over the string if the cards are folded. Just before Christmas, let kids deliver or mail their cards.

REMEMBERING THE BIBLE

Each four- or five-week module focuses on a key Bible verse. The key verse for this module is "For nothing is impossible with God" **(Luke 1:37).**

Following are two activities you may do with your third- and fourth-graders to help them remember this Bible verse and apply it to their lives.

MISSION POSSIBLE

Say: **I'm going to give you a mission to accomplish. Your mission is to say one nice thing to everyone in this room in one minute or less. Do you think you can do it? Let's give it a try. Ready, go!**

After a minute, ask:

● **Were you able to reach everybody? Why or why not**? (No, we didn't have enough time; it was hard to think of things to say; yes, I went as fast as I could; it was easy because we have a small class.)

Say: **We're going to try this mission one more time, but first let's read a verse from the Bible.**

Distribute Bibles and have students look up **Luke 1:37.** When all kids have found the verse, have them read it aloud together. Ask:

● **How does knowing God make you feel?** (Great; glad I believe in God; amazed at God's power.)

● **What are some things God can help you do this week?** (Be nice to my little sister; obey my parents; remember to pray.)

Say: **Let's ask God to help us accomplish our missions.** Pray: **Dear God, We're amazed at your great power. Thank you for helping us accomplish the tasks we could never do alone. Help us spread good and encouraging feelings to everyone in this room now. Amen.**

Form trios. Have each group appoint a sender and two runners. Say: **Senders, your job is to send your runners out to spread good feelings to other people. When you send out a runner, tell him or her exactly what to do. For example, you could say, "Runner, go tell** (name of a boy in the class) **that you're glad he's here today," or "Runner, go tell** (name of a girl in class) **that you like the way she's always kind." Runners, your job is to complete your assignments as quickly as possible and return to the person who sent you. Senders, be ready to give your runners another assignment when they return. Ready, go!**

Repeat the activity two more times to give all kids a chance to be senders. Have kids give one another a round of applause for accomplishing the mission.

Say: **We didn't think our mission was possible, but with God's help, we did it. When you face a hard situation this week, remember: God is on your side, and God can do anything!**

CAN YOU KEEP UP?

Say: **Sometimes it's hard to keep up with everything that's going on at Christmastime. We're going to play a little game now to see how well we can keep up. All you have to do is follow my directions, like you would in Simon Says.**

Read the following list of actions, pausing after each one to allow kids time to respond.

● **Think about the food you'll have for Christmas dinner. Then rub your stomach.**

● **Think about how excited you'll be to open your gifts. Then run in place. But don't stop rubbing your stomach.**

● **Think about how happy you'll be on Christmas day. Then sing "Joy to the World!" But don't stop running in place or rubbing your stomach.**

● **Close your eyes and imagine your Christmas tree. But don't stop singing or running in place or rubbing your stomach.**

● **Think about how tired you'll be by the end of Christmas day. Yawn and pat your mouth. But don't open your eyes. And don't stop singing or running in place or rubbing your stomach.**

Let kids try to perform all five actions for about a minute, then tell them to stop. Have kids sit down and relax. Ask:

● **What was it like trying to do all those actions at the same time?** (Confusing; hard; after a while I got tired from running in place.)

● **What other hard situations do you face in life?** (Making new friends; getting all my homework done; getting along with my family.)

● **How do you handle those hard situations?** (I try to do the best I can; I ask my parents to help me; I pray about them.)

Say: **God can help us with the hard situations we face in life. And if we have God helping us, those situations won't seem quite as hard after all. It says in the Bible that God can do anything. Let's say that together: "For nothing is impossible with God." Say it one more time, louder: "For nothing is impossible with God." Remember this verse when you face a hard situation this week.**

LESSON 1

ANYTHING'S POSSIBLE!

THE POINT

☞ **All things are possible with God.**

THE BIBLE BASIS

Luke 1:5-25, 57-66. John the Baptist is born.

Just before he writes the wondrous account of Jesus' birth, Luke tells another amazing story. God gives an aged, childless couple the baby they've always wanted. What seems impossible actually happens, to the amazement of everyone who hears about it. The story of Zechariah and Elizabeth declares a message that's repeated throughout Luke's gospel: All things are possible with God.

For third- and fourth-graders lots of things seem impossible, from getting along with brothers and sisters to doing well in school. For some, being patient seems impossible. For others, memorizing recital music, running a mile, or learning long division seems like an impossible task. Use this lesson to teach kids that God sees all kinds of possibilities for each of them.

Other Scriptures used in this lesson are **Matthew 18:19-20; Luke 1:13-14, 18; 18:27.**

GETTING THE POINT

Students will
- learn that with God all things are possible,
- imagine "impossible" things God might help them do, and
- think of ways to rely on God in difficult situations.

THIS LESSON AT A GLANCE

Before the lesson, collect the necessary items from the Learning Lab for the activities you plan to use. Refer to the pictures in the margin to see what each item looks like.

SECTION	MINUTES	WHAT STUDENTS WILL DO	LEARNING LAB SUPPLIES	CLASSROOM SUPPLIES
ATTENTION GRABBER	up to 10	**PICTURE THIS!**—Tell teammates good news without speaking.		3x5 cards, markers, paper
BIBLE EXPLORATION AND APPLICATION	up to 15	**WHAT WILL THE NEIGHBORS SAY?**—Read the story of Zechariah and Elizabeth from Luke 1:5-23, 57-66 and describe what happened from the neighbors' points of view.		Bibles, "The Neighbors Are Talking" handout (p. 25), paper, pencils
	up to 11	**CAN YOU GET IT TOGETHER?**—Race to solve an impossible puzzle and read Luke 1:13-14, 18.	Shape puzzles	Bibles
	up to 12	**MISSION IMPOSSIBLE**—Create a strategy to help them face difficult situations and read Matthew 18:19-20 and Luke 18:27.	Cassette: "Mission Impossible"	Bibles, chalkboard and chalk, newsprint and marker, cassette player
CLOSING	up to 12	**IT'S POSSIBLE!**—Write on blank ornaments the things God might help them do.	Top pens, sequin dust, "Trimming the Tree" poster, cassette: "Christmas Music Medley," "Lyrics Poster"	Markers, crayons, construction paper, scissors, tape, cassette player

Remember to make photocopies of the "Hands-On Fun at Home" handout (p. 26) to send home with your kids. The "Fun at Home" handout suggests ways for kids to talk with their families about what they're learning in class and helps them put their faith into action.

THE LESSON

Explain to the kids that whenever you ring the *gold foil bell,* they are to stop talking, raise their hands, and focus on you. Explain that it's important to respond to this signal quickly so the class can do as many fun activities as possible. Practice the signal two or three times.

ATTENTION GRABBER

PICTURE THIS!
(up to 10 minutes)

Form groups of no more than four. Give each group four 3×5 cards, markers, and paper.

Say: **You'll have three minutes to think of some really exciting news you'd like to tell someone right away. It might be something that happened at school or something you got in the mail. Write one example on each of your group's index cards.**

After three minutes, ring the *gold foil bell.* Wait for kids to respond, then have one person from each group collect the cards and exchange them for another group's cards.

Say: **Take turns drawing one of the cards your group received, but don't show that card to anyone else. Each of you will take turns giving clues to your teammates so they can guess the good news that's written on your card. There's only one catch: You can't say or write a word. Use your markers and paper to draw pictures of your good news, or act out the good news without talking. You have five minutes to see how many good news messages your group can guess.**

After five minutes, ring the *gold foil bell.* Wait for kids to respond, then ask any groups who guessed all their good news to stand and take a bow as everyone applauds. Ask:

● **What was it like when you had something important to say but you weren't able to talk or use words?** (It was silly; I was upset; I felt smart, since I found a way to tell my team without talking.)

Say: **Today we're going to read about a man named Zechariah who lost his voice after an angel told him his wife Elizabeth was going to have a baby. For nine months—a whole school year— Zechariah couldn't talk.**

Ask:

● **How was this activity like what happened to Zechariah?** (He had great news to tell, but he couldn't talk; he probably had to draw or act things out to get his messages across.)

Say: **Telling something important without being able to talk may**

TEACHER TIP

Circulate among groups and offer ideas. Encourage kids to speak quietly so other groups don't overhear their discussions. As groups exchange cards, be sure each person will have a new card to draw. You may need to take an extra card from one group and give it to another.

the POINT

have seemed impossible at first. But even without your voices, you were able to communicate your good news to your friends. We should think twice before we say something can't happen. ☞ **Even when things seem impossible to us, all things are possible with God.**

BIBLE EXPLORATION AND APPLICATION

WHAT WILL THE NEIGHBORS SAY?
(up to 15 minutes)

Before class, photocopy the "The Neighbors Are Talking" handout (p. 25) and cut apart the neighborhood assignments. Say: **Let's find out more about what happened to Zechariah and Elizabeth.** Distribute Bibles and ask several volunteers to read **Luke 1:5-20.** Assign each volunteer three to five verses. Have other kids follow along in their Bibles.

Say: **Imagine you're one of Zechariah and Elizabeth's neighbors. One day everything seems normal, and the next day this older couple down the street is going to have a baby! You see this whole story taking place, and you have lots to say about it! After you receive your assignment, you'll have five minutes to read your passage, discuss it, and practice telling your section of the story from the neighbors' points of view.**

Form four "neighborhoods" and give each neighborhood an assignment from the handout, paper, and a pencil. Tell each group to choose a reader to read its Bible passage to the group, a recorder to write responses to the questions, an encourager to urge everyone to participate in the discussion, and a reporter to share the neighborhood's comments with the class.

As students work, be ready to offer help to any groups that may need guidance to complete the assignment.

After five minutes, ring the *gold foil bell* and gather the neighborhood groups in a circle to tell the story. Beginning with Neighborhood A, have the reader read the verses that describe the events his or her neighborhood witnessed. Then have the reporter share the neighbors' reactions. Other group members may help the reporter if he or she omits details. Continue with Neighborhoods B, C, and D. When all the groups have reported, ask:

● **Why do you think people were so interested in Zechariah and Elizabeth's baby?** (Because Zechariah and Elizabeth were too old to have a baby, but they had one anyway; because Zechariah lost his voice.)

● **What do you think people must have thought about God after seeing these things happen?** (That God can do anything; that you never know what God might do; that God is powerful.)

Say: **If people hadn't seen this happen, they might have thought it was impossible. But God did something very special when he gave Zechariah and Elizabeth a baby boy named John. God was making preparations for another amazing birth soon to come, the birth of Jesus. If we didn't know about this story, we might think it was impossible for an older couple to have a baby, too. But because it did happen, we know that** **all things are possible with God.**

CAN YOU GET IT TOGETHER?
(up to 11 minutes)

Form two teams and have each team sit in a circle on the floor.

Say: **The angel's message must have surprised Zechariah. Let's look at that part of the story again.** Ask volunteers to read the angel's message in **Luke 1:13-14,** and Zechariah's response in **Luke 1:18** as other kids follow along in their Bibles.

Say: **The idea of Elizabeth having a baby seemed impossible to Zechariah. His first words to the angel show that he didn't understand how this could happen. I wonder what you'd say if you were asked to do something you thought was impossible.**

Give each team one *shape puzzle.* Say: **When I say "go," one person on each team should grab the *shape puzzle* and begin to take it apart. You'll have 10 seconds to work on the puzzle. When I ring the *gold foil bell* and say "change," you must immediately pass the *shape puzzle* to the next person in the circle.**

If you have a watch with a second hand, use it to time this activity. If you don't have a watch, simply count. Every 10 seconds you should ring the *gold foil bell* and say "change." Give kids each at least three turns at taking the puzzle apart and putting it back together.

After team members have had at least three chances to work on their puzzles, say "switch." Have teams switch puzzles and continue working the same way, passing the puzzle to another team member every 10 seconds. When everyone has had at least three turns with the second *shape puzzle,* stop the game. Collect the *shape puzzles* and place them out of sight for use in future lessons.

Have kids stand up. Say: **Raise your hands when you think of an answer to each question I ask. I'd like to hear lots of different, interesting answers. When someone gives an answer you've thought of and you don't have anything more to add, you may sit down. When everyone is seated, I'll ask you to stand again for the next question.**

TEACHER TIP

It's important to say The Point just as it's written in each activity. Repeating The Point over and over will help kids remember it and apply it to their lives.

 the POINT

LEARNING LAB

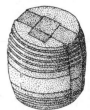

BIBLE *INSIGHT*

Luke alternated the stories of Jesus and John the Baptist as a literary device to link these stories to the prophecies of the Old Testament. In so doing, Luke clearly identified John as a continuance of the prophetic line and Jesus as the promised Messiah.

TEACHER TIP

If kids are interested in solving the *shape puzzles,* make the puzzles available after class.

Ask:

● **What was your reaction when it was your turn to work on the puzzle?** (Confused; worried; I was ready for it to be someone else's turn.)

● **Did you think there was any way you could complete these puzzles? Why or why not?** (No, we didn't have enough time to think about it; no, we had too many people working on it; maybe, because we have smart people in our class.)

● **How is the way you felt about these puzzles like the way Zechariah may have felt when he heard that Elizabeth would have a baby?** (He might have been confused; he didn't understand how that could happen.)

● **What are some ways we could complete these *shape puzzles* if we tried again?** (Give directions next time; talk about how to solve it before we work on it; not race; give each person more time.)

Say: **Sometimes things seem impossible to us, like our impossible puzzle relay. We don't always see how things might work out. We can understand how Zechariah might have felt. But even when things seem impossible to us, all things are possible with God.**

the POINT

LEARNING LAB

TEACHER TIP

If students seem stumped, ask questions such as "What's the hardest thing about making friends?" "What's hard about getting along with people?" "When is it tough to do what your parents say to do?" By asking such questions, you'll help kids think of their own examples.

MISSION IMPOSSIBLE
(up to 12 minutes)

Form a large circle. On a chalkboard or newsprint, write the heading "Impossible Missions" and choose a volunteer to list the group's ideas as they mention them.

Say: **Have you ever said, "That's impossible"? We may think lots of things are so difficult they could never happen. Let's make a list of difficult or impossible situations you might face each day. For example, spending an entire day without arguing with your brother or sister may seem impossible to you. What other impossible situations can you think of?**

Have your volunteer write the ideas on the chalkboard or newsprint. When the list is finished, say: **Just because something's impossible for people doesn't mean it's really impossible. I'll show you what I mean.** Distribute Bibles and ask a volunteer to read **Luke 18:27.** Have other students follow along in their Bibles. Ask:

● **Why do you think God can do things that are impossible for people?** (Because he's God; God is more powerful than people; God knows everything.)

● **What are some ways God can help you do things that seem impossible?** (God can change my heart so I won't get angry at my little sister; God can give me patience when I have to wait for something.)

Form no more than four teams. Say: **Look over our list of impossible situations and pick the three things you think would be the hardest to do. You'll have about two minutes to decide.**

Play the "Mission Impossible" segment of the *cassette tape* as teams are working. When the music stops, call for kids' attention by ringing the *gold foil bell.* Wait for kids to respond, then have a representative from each group put an X next to the situations on the newsprint that his or her group thought were most difficult. Count the number of X's next to each situation, then announce the four most impossible situations. Assign each team one of the four situations. Say: **You've just been assigned to a *Mission Impossible* team. Your assignment is to develop a plan to help us rely on God when we face the situation you've been assigned.**

Distribute markers and newsprint. Have each team choose a recorder who will listen to the team's suggestions and write down its plan and a spokesperson who'll share its plan with the class. Encourage students to choose roles different from those they had in the previous activity.

Say: **You'll have about four minutes to create your plan. Go!**

After three or four minutes, ring the *gold foil bell.* Wait for kids to respond, then form a large circle. Have each team's spokesperson share the team's plan with the class. Then ask:

● **Was it easy or difficult to think of a plan for handling these impossible situations? Explain.** (Easy, there are lots of ways to learn to trust God; difficult, we don't like to face difficult things.)

● **How can God help us handle these impossible situations?** (God will help us know what to say and do; God can make things turn out for the best.)

Say: **Believing that God can do anything can have amazing results in our lives. Listen to what Jesus says about the power of faith.** Have a volunteer read **Matthew 18:19-20** as other kids follow along in their Bibles.

Then ask:

● **What does this passage say about asking God for help?** (We have to ask that God will be with us.)

Say: **Whenever we face a situation that seems impossible to us, we need to remember that we're not alone. All things are possible with God, and we can pray and ask God to help us. Find a partner and take a moment to pray for the impossible situations you talked about with your teams.**

Give kids a minute or two to pray for their situations, then close by saying "amen."

 the POINT

We believe that Christian education extends beyond the classroom into the home. Photocopy the "Hands-On Fun at Home" handout (p. 26) for this week and send it home with your kids. Encourage kids to try several activities and discuss the Bible verses and questions with their parents.

> **TEACHER TIP**
> To enhance this activity, you might want to play the role of a secret agent, complete with trench coat, sunglasses, and briefcase. When you hand teams their newsprint, you could take it out of a file labeled "Top Secret."

LEARNING LAB

the POINT ✍

Set out the *top pens* and the *sequin dust* and distribute construction paper, markers, crayons, and scissors. Be sure to reserve some *sequin dust* for use in future lessons. Hold up the "Trimming the Tree" poster from the Learning Lab. Say: **Make an ornament for the tree and write on it one "impossible" thing you'd like God to help you do, either by yourself or with others in our class. If you need help thinking of a situation, choose one from the list we made in the last activity. If you want to make more than one ornament, that's OK.**

As kids are working, tape the "Trimming the Tree" poster in a prominent location in your classroom. Give kids up to 10 minutes to decorate their ornaments, then ring the *gold foil bell*. Wait for kids to respond, then have them take turns reading their ornaments to the class and "hanging" them on the poster. Help kids attach their ornaments to the tree by using tape or a glue stick. As kids are attaching their ornaments to the poster, lead the rest of the class in cheering, "With God's help, you can do it!"

When all the ornaments are attached to the poster, play the "Christmas Music Medley" segment of the *cassette tape* and sing along with the music. (The words are on the "Lyrics Poster" found in the Learning Lab.) Collect the *top pens* and *sequin dust* for use in later lessons.

Explain that if kids think of other things they'd like God to help them do over the next few weeks, they can continue to make and add ornaments to the tree.

Say: **Sometimes we focus on seeing all the things we can't do. But God sees all the things we can do with his help. God sees all kinds of possibilities in people. ✍ All things are possible with God.**

THE NEIGHBORS ARE TALKING

Neighborhood A

Read **Luke 1:21-23.** You are the people standing outside the temple when Zechariah came out.

- How did you know something had happened to Zechariah?
- What did you think when Zechariah couldn't talk?

Neighborhood B

Read **Luke 1:57-58.** You are the neighbors who rejoiced.

- What did you say to each other when Elizabeth's baby was born?
- Why were you so happy?

Neighborhood C

Read **Luke 1:59-63.** You are the people who were at the scene as the baby was being named.

- What was surprising about the baby's name?
- What did you say when Elizabeth chose the name John?

Neighborhood D

Read **Luke 1:64-66.** You were there when Zechariah began to talk again.

- What kinds of things did you hear him say?
- What did you think when Zechariah began to talk again?

Hands-On FUN! AT HOME

BIBLE FOCUS

"For nothing is impossible with God"
(Luke 1:37).

WAY to PRAY

Give family members each a sheet of white paper and have them fold and cut into a paper snowflake. When you've finished cutting your snowflakes, have each person in your family name a difficult situation he or she might fact this week and write it on a snowflake. For example, maybe someone is taking a hard project at work or school, or someone needs to apologize for something or she has done wrong. Hang the snowflakes on your Christmas tree to remind you to pray for one another.

POSSIBILITIES

Practice seeing new possibilities by playing this game. Choose three or four common objects in your house such as a spoon, a box, a sock, and an envelope. Let everyone take turns suggesting different ways they might use each object. Name as many new possibilities for each object as you can. Then go on to the next object. Finish by naming something you think each of your family members might do well someday.

FAITH walk

"Adopt" someone who's alone in your community this Christmas season. Check with your church or community agencies for names of people who don't have families living nearby. Talk about ways your family could show God's love to those people. Plan to do something for or with that person once a week during the Christmas season.

NOTables

Ask each person in your family to fill out a list like the one below. One night after dinner, share your lists as a family. Then celebrate God's faithfulness by having an ice cream "praise party"!

GOD + ME = POSSIBILITY!

What possibilities do you think God might have in mind for you?

_____

_____

_____

_____

_____

LESSON

2

WHO, ME?

THE POINT

God uses ordinary people.

THE BIBLE BASIS

Luke 1:26-45. An angel appears to Mary.

An angel visits a young, small-town woman with the message that she will give birth to the Savior of the world. Our extraordinary God calls upon an ordinary person. By choosing Mary as the mother of Jesus, God made it clear that his kingdom does not depend on the people and values that the world considers important. God uses ordinary people.

Many 8- and 9-year-olds spend lots of time feeling ordinary, wondering if there is anything special about them. They're sandwiched between kids who are fresh out of preschool, and kids who are almost teenagers. They're given more responsibilities than younger children and fewer privileges than older children. Your students need to know that they're special people and that God can use them just as they are. For third- and fourth-graders who want to be somebody, but feel just ordinary, this lesson is good news!

Other Scriptures used in this lesson are **Matthew 1:18-21** and **1 Thessalonians 5:11.**

GETTING THE POINT

Students will

● understand that God uses ordinary people,

● discuss and understand that God will use them if they are willing, and

● learn that God can use them to encourage others.

THIS LESSON AT A GLANCE

Before the lesson, collect the necessary items from the Learning Lab for the activities you plan to use. Refer to the pictures in the margin to see what each item looks like.

SECTION	MINUTES	WHAT STUDENTS WILL DO	LEARNING LAB SUPPLIES	CLASSROOM SUPPLIES
ATTENTION GRABBER	up to 10	**WILL YOU RISK IT?**—Decide whether to accept an assignment that leads to a risk, a reward, or both.	Neon loops	"Will You Risk It?" handouts (p. 35), envelopes, treats
BIBLE EXPLORATION AND APPLICATION	up to 15	**MUSICAL VERSES**—Play a musical game and discuss Luke 1:26-38 and Matthew 1:18-21.	Cassette: "Angels We Have Heard on High"	Bibles, cassette player
	up to 15	**GOD COULD USE US!**—Invent news stories about ways God might use kids and read Luke 1:28-29.	Cassette: "In the News"	Bibles, paper, pencils, cassette player
	up to 15	**THAT'S ENCOURAGING**—Read Luke 1:39-45 and 1 Thessalonians 5:11 and write notes of encouragement to classmates.	Paper streamer roll, metallic ribbons	Bible, scissors, markers
CLOSING	up to 5	**OH, THE THINGS GOD CAN DO WITH ME AND WITH YOU!**—Name things they'll do for God and others.	Pine cone	

Hands-On FUN AT HOME Remember to make photocopies of the "Hands-On Fun at Home" handout (p. 36) to send home with your kids. The "Fun at Home" handout suggests ways for kids to talk with their families about what they're learning in class and helps them put their faith into action.

THE LESSON

As kids arrive, ask them which "Fun at Home" activities they tried. Ask questions such as "What situations did your family pray about last week?" and "How did your family show God's love to someone else?"

Explain to the kids that whenever you ring the *gold foil bell*, they are to stop talking, raise their hands, and focus on you. Explain that it's important to respond to this signal quickly so the class can do as many fun activities as possible.

ATTENTION GRABBER

WILL YOU RISK IT?
(up to 10 minutes)

LEARNING LAB

Before class, photocopy the "Will You Risk It?" handout (p. 35) and cut the assignments apart. Make enough copies so that each student will have an assignment. Put each assignment in a separate envelope with a *neon loop.* Seal the envelopes.

Say: **You're invited to take a risk today. I have an envelope for each of you. You don't have to take it, but if you do, you must agree to do whatever the instructions inside the envelope ask you to do. If you take this risk, you may also be rewarded. Who wants an envelope?**

Distribute the envelopes. Have kids open their envelopes, complete their assignments, then give you their loops. When kids turn in their loops, give them each a treat. Place the *neon loops* out of sight for use in future lessons. Ask:

● **What thoughts went through your mind when you took an envelope?** (I was curious to find out what was inside; I was afraid it might be a trick.)

● **If you took an envelope, why did you decide to take a risk?** (I thought it would be fun; I hoped there was a good reward.)

● **If you didn't take an envelope, why did you decide not to take a risk?** (I thought it might not be worth it; I didn't care if I got a reward.)

● **What other risks do you take sometimes?** (Volunteering to do a job for someone; trying to be someone's friend.)

● **How was this activity like other risks you might take?** (You never know exactly how it will turn out; if you don't take the risk, you might miss the reward.)

Say: **In our activity, you had to take a risk before you got a reward. At first, some of the opportunities we have to serve God may seem a little risky to us. But the rewards of doing what God wants us to do can be wonderful. ☞ God uses ordinary people like you and me to do important things for him. Today we'll learn**

TEACHER TIP

It's important to say The Point just as it's written in each activity. Repeating The Point over and over will help kids remember it and apply it to their lives.

 **the POINT**

how God used an ordinary young woman to bring his Son into the world.

BIBLE EXPLORATION AND APPLICATION

LEARNING LAB

MUSICAL VERSES
(up to 15 minutes)

Set chairs in a circle. Place a Bible with a bookmark at **Luke 1:26-38** under one chair. Have students stand inside the circle of chairs. Say: **You don't have to be rich or famous for God to use you. Listen while I read Luke 1:26-27. This passage tells about Mary, the mother of Jesus.** Read **Luke 1:26-27** aloud. Say: **Jesus' mother, Mary, wasn't very old—possibly a young teenager. Most people didn't know Mary or her family. But God chose Mary for the special purpose of giving birth to Jesus.**

Play the first "Angels We Have Heard on High" segment from the *cassette tape*. As the music is playing, say: **An angel told Mary she would give birth to Jesus. Let's play a game to find out more about Mary. Whenever you hear the music, walk around the inside of the circle. When the music stops, sit down in the nearest chair.**

Play the second "Angels We Have Heard on High" segment from the *cassette tape*. When the music stops, turn off the tape and say: **If you have a Bible under your chair, you're our designated reader. Open the Bible to the marker and read Luke 1:28-29 aloud.**

After the student reads the verses, say: **When Mary first saw the angel, she was confused and wondered what was going on. Imagine that an angel just appeared to you.** Ask:

● **What's the first thing you might think if you saw an angel?** (I'd be scared; I would wonder if it was a dream.)

Place the Bible under a different chair. Play the third "Angels We Have Heard on High" segment from the *cassette tape* as kids walk around the inside of the circle. When the music stops, turn off the tape, identify the designated reader, and have that student read **Luke 1:30-33** aloud. Then ask the class:

● **How do you think Mary might have felt after hearing the angel's message?** (Excited; happy to be chosen; curious about how it would happen.)

Place the Bible under a different chair. Play the fourth "Angels We Have Heard on High" segment from the *cassette tape* as kids walk around the inside of the circle. When the music stops, turn off the tape, identify the designated reader, and have that student read **Luke 1:34-38** aloud.

After the student reads the verses, ask the class:

● **Do you think you would have agreed to do what the angel said as Mary did? Explain.** (Yes, I'd do what God wanted me to do; no, I might have said, "Let me think this over first.")

● **Why do you think God chose Mary to be Jesus' mother?**
(Because she followed God; because she was nice; God knew she'd make a good mother.)

Place the Bible under another chair. Play the fifth "Angels We Have Heard on High" segment as kids walk around the circle. When the music stops, turn off the tape, identify the designated reader, and have that student read **Matthew 1:18-21** aloud. Then ask the class:

● **Why do you think God chose Joseph to act as Jesus' father?**
(Because he was a kind man; because God trusted him.)

Say: **God could have chosen someone famous, someone important, or someone wealthy to bring his Son into the world. But he didn't. Instead, God chose an unknown young woman who was willing to be his servant. God knew Mary would be a wonderful mother for Jesus and that Joseph would be a good earthly father. God didn't care how famous or important Mary and Joseph were because** **God uses ordinary people. Let's hear how God used another ordinary person.**

 GOD COULD USE US!
(up to 15 minutes)

Say: **We've already heard how God chose Mary to be the mother of Jesus. But how did Mary react to the news? Let's look at Luke 1:28-29 again to find out.**

Have students follow along in their Bibles as you read **Luke 1:28-29** aloud. Say: **In these verses, Mary is confused about why God has chosen her and what the angel's message might mean. Mary might have felt too young or unimportant for such a special task. Tell us about a time you thought you were too young to have something special happen to you.** (My sister said summer camp was really fun, but I was too young to go; my brother gets to drive, but it'll be zillions of years before I can drive.)

Say: **God uses ordinary people, and God can use kids, too. We're going to hear a true story now about a boy whose special actions made news headlines.**

Play the "In the News" segment of the *cassette tape.*

Say: **That story is a real example of how an ordinary 11-year-old boy made a difference in the world. If you'd like to know more about Trevor's story, you can read the book** *Trevor's Place,* **written by Trevor's parents, Frank and Janet Ferrell.**

If you're running short on time, you may want to skip the following group activity and move on to "That's Encouraging" on page 32.

Form teams of no more than five. (Teams can be as small as three students.) Give each team paper and a pencil. Have teams choose a writer to record the group's news story, a reporter to present the story to the class, and one or more encouragers to help team members come up with ideas.

 **BIBLE** *INSIGHT*

It's important to note that Joseph tried to solve the dilemma of Mary's pregnancy on his own at first by giving her a secret divorce. It was only afterward that the angel came to Joseph in his dream to solicit his cooperation; thus, the evidence of divine intervention is clear.

 the POINT

LEARNING LAB

 the POINT

Say: **With your team, take about five minutes to invent a story like Trevor's that could happen to someone your age who wants to make a difference for God.**

Have one person on your team begin with a sentence such as "Today a 9-year-old girl made the news." Then take turns adding sentences to your story until everyone has had at least one turn to add a sentence. After everyone has contributed to the story, you can agree to change the details if you want. Have the writer in your group write down the main ideas of the story for the reporter to present to the class.

Circulate among groups and offer ideas to help kids get started. After five minutes, ring the *gold foil bell*. Wait for kids to respond, then have teams present their stories to the class.

When the "newscast" is over, thank everyone for "tuning in." Then ask:

● **Do you think the stories you invented could really happen? Why or why not?** (No, we just tried to make a good story; yes, people can make a big difference if they try.)

● **Would you be willing to do something like the characters in your stories did? Explain.** (Yes, I'd love to help people in a special way; no, I wouldn't know what to do; I'm not sure I could do that.)

Say: **Like Mary, we may wonder why God would want to use us. We may feel awkward and nervous about doing something like what Trevor did. But if we're willing to get involved, God can use us in amazing ways. We know that** **God uses ordinary people—people like you and me.**

TEACHER TIP

To enhance kids' presentations, you may want to play the role of a news anchor. Welcome the class to your newscast and introduce the reporters by name as you ask for their news stories.

the POINT

LEARNING LAB

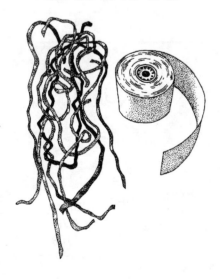

📖 THAT'S ENCOURAGING
(up to 15 minutes)

Say: **Mary wasn't the only person who knew how special her baby would be. Listen to what Elizabeth, Mary's relative, said.**

Have kids look up **Luke 1:39-45.** Ask one volunteer to read the narration in verses 39-41 and another volunteer to read Elizabeth's words to Mary, beginning with verse 42 and ending with verse 45. Have other kids follow along in their Bibles. When the readers finish, ask:

● **How do you think Elizabeth made Mary feel?** (Special; happy; honored.)

● **How do you feel when someone encourages you?** (Like I can do something special; like I have a friend; more confident.)

● **What kinds of encouraging things could we say to each other?** ("You're a good friend"; "you're smart"; we could tell people what they do well.)

Cut a foot-long piece of the *paper streamer roll* for each person, including yourself. Distribute the paper streamer pieces and markers and have kids write their names on one side of their streamers.

Say: **Let's check out what the Bible says about encouragement.**

Have kids look up **1 Thessalonians 5:11.** When all kids have found the passage, ask a volunteer to read it. Say: **We're going to do what this verse says and spend the next five minutes having an encouragement party. Trade papers with someone else and write a note of encouragement to that person on the blank side of the streamer. Keep swapping with different people until you hear the signal. Hold on to the streamer you have when time is called, even if it's not your own.**

At the end of five minutes, ring the *gold foil bell*. Wait for kids to respond, then give each person one *metallic ribbon*. Have kids roll up their streamers and tie them like diplomas with the *metallic ribbons*. When kids have finished wrapping their notes, ask them each to pray silently for the person whose note they're holding. Then have them present the notes to those people.

Give kids a minute or so to open their "diplomas," then collect the *metallic ribbons* and place them out of sight for use in future lessons. Ring the *gold foil bell* and wait for the kids to respond. Ask:

● **What did you learn about encouraging others from this experience?** (Sometimes it's hard to know what to say; it makes people feel good; people like you when you encourage them.)

● **How do you think God feels when we take time to encourage one another?** (God likes us to encourage people; God wants us to encourage others more often.)

Say: **When a friend or family member encourages us, they remind us how special and important we are. We go from feeling ordinary to feeling special. Just as God used Elizabeth to encourage Mary,  God uses ordinary people to spread encouragement to others.**

the POINT

LEARNING LAB

the POINT

TEACHER TIP

If you have a large class, add the other two *pine cones* and pass them around the circle also. At the end of each sentence, have all three people holding *pine cones* give their examples.

OH, THE THINGS GOD CAN DO WITH ME AND WITH YOU!
(up to 5 minutes)

Have kids sit in a circle. Practice saying the words, "Oh, the things God can do with me and with you," together. Say: **I'm going to pass a *pine cone* around the circle as we recite this sentence together. If you're holding the *pine cone* at the end of the sentence, you must name one way God might use you this week.**

After everyone has had an opportunity to participate, retrieve the *pine cone* and place it out of sight for use in future lessons.

Say: **When we choose to serve God, God can use us to do extraordinary things. As you look for ways to serve others this week, remember that** God uses ordinary people. God used Mary, God used Trevor, and God can use you!

WILL YOU RISK IT?

Your assignment is to tell three people why you're glad they're here today. When you've completed your task, take the loop from your envelope and give it to your teacher.

Congratulations on taking this risk!

Your assignment is to pat three people on the back and give them each a big smile. When you've completed your task, take the loop from your envelope and give it to your teacher.

Congratulations on taking this risk!

Your assignment is to say to three people, "It's a great day to be alive! Gimme five!" and give them each a high five. When you've completed your task, take the loop from your envelope and give it to your teacher.

Congratulations on taking this risk!

Your assignment is to shake hands with three people and say, "It's a special day, and you're a special person." When you've completed your task, take the loop from your envelope and give it to your teacher.

Congratulations on taking this risk!

Hands-On FUN! AT HOME

the POINT ☞ **God uses ordinary people.**

■ ■ ■ ■ ■ ■ ■ ■ ■ ■ ■ ■ ■ ■ ■

BIBLE FOCUS

"For nothing is impossible with God" (Luke 1:37).

CHECK it OUT

Read Luke 1:28.
Give an example of a time when you knew God was with you.

Read Luke 1:38.
What would you like to do for God? Name a way you could serve God.

JUST because . . .

Let God use you to encourage members of your family. Fill in this coupon, or make your own, to surprise someone with a thoughtful gesture, such as "one big hug," "help with the dishes," or "one high five."

WHO, me?

Play a game to tell your family members how special they are. Gather pencils and index cards or small pieces of paper. On each card write something one of your family members does well or something you like about that person. Make several cards for everyone in your family. Your parents or brothers and sisters might have fun making these, too.

When you finish your cards, put them in a stack. Take turns drawing cards and guessing who each card describes. After the game, share a group hug!

FAITH walk

Make a scrapbook to show how your family is learning to serve God. Staple several sheets of paper together and decorate the cover, or buy an empty scrapbook or photo album. Include pictures that show members of your family serving others. Or tape or glue things in your book that remind you of ways your family serves God. For example, you might put a leaf in your book to remind you of how you raked a neighbor's yard. Be sure to include a list of things your family might do to serve in the future. Review your scrapbook often to help you remember to serve God.

To: _____ From: _____

This coupon good for...

_____

just because you're you!

LESSON 3

GOD'S SON IS BORN

"For nothing is impossible with God"

(Luke 1:37).

THE POINT

Jesus is God's Son.

THE BIBLE BASIS

Luke 2:1-20. Jesus is born in Bethlehem.

Mary and Joseph knew Jesus would be God's gift to the world. But after a long journey, trouble with their hotel plans, the experience of delivering a baby, and making a cradle from a feeding box, they could easily have lost sight of the mystery and excitement of Jesus' birth. The shepherds came along at just the right time to remind them that the baby Jesus lying in the manger was in fact the Son of God.

Like Mary and Joseph, the third- and fourth-graders in your class know that Jesus is God's Son. But schoolwork, friendships, sports, or music lessons may often crowd out kids' relationship with Jesus. In their hectic world, kids need to be reminded that Jesus' birth is much more than a story they've already heard. This lesson will help your students experience the mystery and wonder of Jesus' birth and explore the impact it can have on their lives.

GETTING THE POINT

Students will

● understand that Jesus is God's Son,
● learn that they need to make room for Jesus in their lives, and
● offer thanks to God for sending Jesus.

THIS LESSON AT A GLANCE

Before the lesson, collect the necessary items from the Learning Lab for the activities you plan to use. Refer to the pictures in the margin to see what each item looks like.

SECTION	MINUTES	WHAT STUDENTS WILL DO	LEARNING LAB SUPPLIES	CLASSROOM SUPPLIES
ATTENTION GRABBER	up to 10	**HOW MANY DAYS 'TIL CHRISTMAS?**—List holiday activities and discuss making time for Jesus.	Gold foil bell	"Christmas To-Do List" handouts (p. 46), pencils
BIBLE EXPLORATION AND APPLICATION	up to 10	**NO ROOM**—Squeeze into "inns" and decide when the inns are full, then read Luke 2:1-7.	Paper streamer roll	Bibles, chairs, tape, scissors, paper, markers
	up to 15	**SHEPHERD'S RELAY**—Hurry to reach a goal and read Luke 2:8-16.	Neon loops	Bibles, masking tape
	up to 15	**GO TELL...EVERYONE!**—Discuss Luke 2:17-20 and celebrate Jesus' birth by singing a song.	Cassette: "Go Tell It on the Mountain," "Lyrics Poster"	Bibles, cassette player
CLOSING	up to 10	**MAKING A BED**—Name ways to serve Jesus while lining a "manger."	Metallic ribbons, Learning Lab box	

Hands-On FUN AT HOME

Remember to make photocopies of the "Hands-On Fun at Home" handout (p. 47) to send home with your kids. The "Fun at Home" handout suggests ways for kids to talk with their families about what they're learning in class and helps them put their faith into action.

THE LESSON

As kids arrive, ask them which "Fun at Home" activities they tried. Ask questions such as "What pictures did you put in your family scrapbook?" and "Who did you give an encouragement coupon to last week?"

Explain to the kids that whenever you ring the *gold foil bell,* they are to stop talking, raise their hands, and focus on you. Explain that it's important to respond to this signal quickly so the class can do as many fun activities as possible.

ATTENTION GRABBER

HOW MANY DAYS 'TIL CHRISTMAS?
(up to 10 minutes)

Form a circle. Have a volunteer stand in the middle and hold the *gold foil bell.*

Say to the volunteer: **Think of all the things you need to do before Christmas. Maybe you have to finish shopping or help your mom bake Christmas cookies. Maybe you're going to a party or Christmas program. Wait for me to say "go," then tell the group one thing you need to do to get ready for Christmas. Then toss the *gold foil bell* to someone in the circle.**

Say to the whole class: **When you catch the bell, name something else you need to do before Christmas and toss the bell to someone else. You can't repeat what someone else has said. If you catch the *gold foil bell* and can't think of something right away, we'll all say, "How many days 'til Christmas?" If you can't think of something by the end of the sentence, you can stand in the middle and toss the bell to someone else. Try to keep the game going by thinking of as many different things as you can.**

Continue playing the game until everyone has named at least one thing to do before Christmas. When the game is over, collect the *gold foil bell* and have kids sit in the circle. Give each person a copy of the "Christmas To-Do List" handout (p. 46) and a pencil.

Say: **We've just named lots of things to do before Christmas. Think about all the things there are to do, and imagine you only have enough time to do five of them before Christmas. If you have trouble thinking of things, use the examples on your handout. You'll have three minutes to make a list of the top five things you need to do before Christmas Day.**

After three minutes, ring the *gold foil bell.* Wait for kids to respond, then ask:

● **How did it feel to try to squeeze everything you need to do**

GOD'S SON IS BORN

before Christmas into one small list? (Upsetting; frustrating; terrible—I couldn't do everything I wanted to do.)

Help kids form pairs. Say: **Tell your partner which activity was #1 on your list and why that activity was most important.** After partners have shared, continue: **Now look at your list and see how many of your activities include spending time with Jesus to celebrate his birth. Share your discoveries with your partner.**

Give kids a few moments to look over their lists and talk with partners, then ring the *gold foil bell* to regain their attention. Have kids report their discoveries to the class, then ask:

● **What's your favorite Christmas activity?** (Shopping for presents; decorating the tree; singing Christmas carols.)

● **How do we choose activities to celebrate Christmas?** (By doing what our family is doing; we pick the things that seem the most fun; by starting with what we have to get done, like buying presents for other people.)

● **Why is it sometimes hard to focus on Jesus during the Christmas season?** (Because we have a lot of special activities going on; because we spend too much time worrying about decorations and presents.)

● **How can we make better choices to keep Jesus at the center of Christmas?** (By going to church on Christmas before opening presents; by remembering the real meaning of Christmas.)

Say: **With all the activity that goes on at Christmastime, it's easy to get so busy that we forget to make time for Jesus.**  **Jesus is God's Son, and his birth is the reason we celebrate Christmas. We're going to learn more about the importance of Jesus' birth today.**

the POINT

LEARNING LAB

BIBLE EXPLORATION AND APPLICATION

NO ROOM
(up to 10 minutes)

Before students arrive, prepare for the "No Room" activity by setting up several "inns" in an open area of the classroom. For each inn, place two chairs back to back, about 2 feet apart. Cut or tear off two 2-foot lengths of the *paper streamer roll*. Tape the ends of the streamer pieces to the edges of both chairs, as shown in the margin illustration.

Each inn should hold no more than four kids. If you have fewer than eight students in your class, set the chairs closer together so each inn holds only three students. Set up only enough inns to house about three-fourths of your class. Place a sheet of paper and a marker on one of the chairs at each inn. Ask:

● **Where does your family stay when you go on a long trip?** (In a tent; in a hotel; with relatives or friends.)

● **Can you tell about a time when you were unable to find a place to stay? What did your family do?** (We had to keep driving for a long time; we slept in the car; once we stayed in a church.)

Say: **Imagine it's a holiday weekend and you're going on a trip with your family. You're tired because you've been in the car all day. It's getting dark, and now you're helping your parents look for a place to stay. Finally, you see motels in the distance** (point out the "inns" you've made). **You want to stay in one of those motels, but so does everyone else driving along the freeway.**

When I say "go," crawl to one of the inns and stand inside. Whatever you do, don't break through the paper-streamer "walls." If the walls break, no one will be able to use that inn. When everyone inside the inn agrees that it's full, one person in the inn should make a "No Room" sign to hold up. That inn is then closed. You'll have one minute to find a place to stay. Go!

When all the inns are closed, ring the *gold foil bell.* Have kids leave the inns and return to the seats they had before the game.

Ask:

● **How did you feel when you got to an inn and it was closed?** (Disappointed; angry; worried.)

● **What did you think when you had found a place in an inn, but your friends didn't have anywhere to stay?** (I wanted to squeeze them in with us; I was glad I got a place so fast; I felt sorry for them.)

Say: **When Mary and Joseph got to Bethlehem, they couldn't find a place to stay either. Listen to how God took care of them.** Distribute Bibles and have kids look up **Luke 2:1-7.** Have a volunteer read the passage aloud as other kids follow along in their Bibles. Ask:

● **How was our activity like what happened to Mary and Joseph just before Jesus was born?** (There wasn't any room for them in the inn at Bethlehem; they might have been worried when they didn't have a place for Jesus to be born; no one tried to make room for them.)

Say: **Sometimes we're so busy with activities in our lives, such as sports, music, school, or church events, that we don't have room for Jesus.** Ask:

● **How can you make room for Jesus in your life?** (By going to church more; by reading the Bible before I go to bed; by praying.)

Say: **Because 📖 Jesus is God's Son, we might think people would have made special preparations for his birth, like providing a comfortable place for Mary to rest and have the baby. Instead, Mary and Joseph weren't even given a room in the inn. Mary had to lay her baby in a box where animals are fed. But in spite of the humble surroundings, people came from far away to worship God's Son. Let's hear about some of those people now.**

"For nothing is impossible with God" (Luke 1:37).

Kids often overlook the importance of Jesus' birth because they are so familiar with the story. Use the Key Verse to teach them that Jesus' birth was a wondrous miracle made possible by God.

🖎 the POINT

LEARNING LAB

TEACHER TIP

If you have a large room, put the masking tape lines further apart or do this activity outside on the church lawn or parking lot.

TEACHER TIP

Encourage active participation in the discussion by following up kids' answers with questions such as "What did you mean by that?" and "Can you tell me more?"

SHEPHERD'S SLINGSHOT RELAY
(up to 15 minutes)

Form two teams and have teams sit in two straight lines facing each other. Say: **In Bible times, shepherds stayed outside all night long to watch their sheep. The Bible tells us about some very special shepherds.** Distribute Bibles and help kids look up **Luke 2:8-16.** Ask the first person in one line to read verse 8 aloud. Then have the first person in the other line read verse 9. Have kids continue reading the verses, alternating teams, until they've read all nine verses.

Say: **The shepherds in our story hurried to Bethlehem to see Jesus. Let's see what hurrying might have been like by having a shepherd's relay.**

Make two masking tape lines on the floor, about 10 feet apart. Give kids each a *neon loop* and have them line up in their teams behind one of the lines.

Say: **Pretend you've just been given a shepherd's slingshot. To shoot your slingshot, hold the front part of the loop with your thumb, pull back the other end of the loop with your other hand, and let go. Let's try that once or twice.**

Let kids practice shooting their slingshots, then ring the *gold foil bell* to regain their attention. Wait for them to respond, then say: **When it's your turn, shoot your slingshot, hurry to the place it lands, pick it up, and shoot it again. Keep going until you reach the other masking tape line, then hurry back to your team and tag the next person in line. When I see that everyone on your team has finished, I'll ring the *gold foil bell*, and your team may sit down.**

When both teams have finished the relay, applaud the team that finished first and let its members take a bow.

Say: **Now find a partner who has the same color *neon loop*. Discuss the following questions with your partner.**

Pause after you ask each of the following questions to give pairs time for discussion. Ask:

● **What feelings did you have as you hurried to shoot your slingshot to the finish line?** (I felt worried because my slingshot kept backfiring; I felt excited because I was in a hurry; I felt good because I knew I could help my team win.)

● **How are those feelings like the shepherds' feelings as they hurried to find baby Jesus?** (They might have been a little scared; they were probably excited to see Jesus.)

● **Why do you think God picked the shepherds to be the first people to hear about Jesus' birth?** (Maybe they believed in God; they were nearby; they were the only ones awake so late at night.)

● **Why do you think God sent angels to announce Jesus' birth?** (Because it was really important; God wanted to make sure he got people's attention; to celebrate.)

● **The angels said that the news of Jesus' birth would bring great joy to all the people; why was Jesus' birth such good news?** (Because it showed people that God cared enough to send his Son; because it was the first Christmas.)

Call for kids' attention by ringing the *gold foil bell.* Wait for kids to respond, then collect the *neon loops* and place them out of sight for use in future lessons. Invite kids to share the answers they discussed with their partners.

Say: **People had been waiting for God's Son to come to earth for many years. Long ago, the Old Testament prophets predicted that God would send a Savior to take the punishment for all the wrong things people have done. When the angels announced, "Today your Savior was born in the town of David," the shepherds knew Jesus was the promised Savior they'd been waiting for.**

They immediately left to check out this exciting news. They didn't stop to worry about what would happen to their sheep. They didn't care that it was the middle of the night. They knew that **Jesus is God's Son, and they wanted to put him first in their lives.**

the POINT

BIBLE *INSIGHT*

There could be several reasons God picked shepherds to hear the good news first. Because shepherds had a low social status, the implication is that God intentionally chose social outcasts to first hear the gospel. It also correlates with David's calling from shepherd life (2 Samuel 7:8). Shepherds are also symbolic (in both Testaments) as those who care for God's people.

GO TELL... EVERYONE!
(up to 15 minutes)

Say: **Seeing the angels and worshiping Jesus was probably the most exciting thing that ever happened to those shepherds.** Ask:

● **What's the best, most exciting thing that's ever happened to you?** (When we visited my grandparents; when I got a new baby sister; when we went to Disneyland.)

● **What did you do when that exciting thing happened?** (I told everybody; I cried; I jumped up and down.)

● **Imagine you were able to meet Jesus face to face; what would you do?** (Clean up; be scared; take my Bible.)

Say: **Well, God's people in biblical times had waited for the promised Savior for many years—even whole lifetimes. Let's find out how they responded to the news of Jesus' birth and the chance to see Jesus face to face.**

Distribute Bibles and have kids look up **Luke 2:17-20.** After all kids have found the passage, ask a volunteer to read it. Have kids stand as you explain the activity. Say: **I'm going to ask a few questions. Raise your hands when you've thought of an answer to each question. I'd like to hear lots of different, interesting answers, so I'll wait until all of you have thought of answers. When someone gives an answer you've thought of and you don't have anything more to add, you may sit down. When everyone is seated, I'll ask you to stand again for the next question.** Ask:

● **What do you think people thought when they heard the shepherds' story?** (They probably thought the shepherds were crazy; they

LEARNING LAB

might have wanted to go to Bethlehem and see for themselves; they were probably excited that the promised Savior had finally come.)

● **If you had been a listener back then, what part of the shepherds' story would you have found the most amazing?** (I'd wonder if the shepherds dreamed the part about all the angels; that a baby could be their Savior.)

● **The shepherds were so excited that they probably told everyone they met about Jesus' birth; who would you tell about Jesus' birth?** (My parents; my friends at school; my teachers.)

● **What's the most important thing you'd want those people to know about Jesus?** (That Jesus loves them; that Jesus is God's Son; that Christmas is a celebration of Jesus' birth.)

Say: **Although we didn't see Jesus in the manger like the shepherds did, his birth can still change our lives.**  **Jesus is God's Son, and because Jesus came to earth, we can all be part of God's family. Let's sing a song to celebrate that now.**

Lead kids in singing the first verse of "Go Tell It on the Mountain" with the *cassette tape*. The lyrics are printed on the "Lyrics Poster" in the Learning Lab.

Say: **As we sing the rest of the verses, we're going to change the chorus. Instead of singing, "Go tell it on the mountain," I'll sing, "Go tell** (name a student in your class)**." Instead of singing, "Over the hills and ev'rywhere," I'll sing two or three more names. When I sing "Go tell" the second time, I'll add some more names. Each time I sing a person's name, give that person a high five to show you're glad Jesus came for him or her.**

After the song, gather kids in a circle and say: **Let's thank God for sending his Son Jesus to us.**

Pray: **Dear God, thank you for sending your Son Jesus to earth so we can be part of your family. Help us remember to spend time with Jesus as we celebrate his birth this Christmas season. In Jesus' name, amen.**

the POINT 👉

TEACHER TIP

If you're uncomfortable singing alone, try shouting out kids' names instead. Or have kids take turns calling out names each time you sing the chorus.

Hands-On FUN AT HOME

We believe that Christian education extends beyond the classroom into the home. Photocopy the "Hands-On Fun at Home" handout (p. 47) for this week and send it home with your kids. Encourage kids to try several activities and discuss the Bible verses and questions with their parents.

CLOSING

MAKING A BED
(up to 10 minutes)

Place the Learning Lab box in the center of the circle you formed for the last activity. Give each student two or three *metallic ribbons.*

Say: **Mary and Joseph had to make a bed for Jesus by using a feed box. We're going to make our own manger by lining the Learning Lab box with *metallic ribbons.* Think of something you could do to serve Jesus this Christmas. Maybe you'll serve Jesus by giving a small gift to a homeless shelter or children's home. Maybe you'll serve Jesus by doing your chores without complaining. When you think of a way to serve Jesus, share your idea with the class, then put your ribbon in the box to represent your idea.**

If kids can think of only one idea, have them put all their ribbons in the box at once. If they have several ideas, have them share an idea for each ribbon. Continue the activity until all the ribbons are in the box, then say: **We celebrate Christmas to remember Jesus' birth and to remember that Jesus is God's Son. When we think about how great it is that God sent Jesus, it's easy to remember to spend time serving Jesus.**

Keep the Learning Lab box and *metallic ribbons* for use in future lessons.

the POINT

Christmas To-Do List

Think of all the things you need to do before Christmas. Imagine you have time to do only five of these things before December 25. List the top five things you'd put on your "Christmas To-Do List." Number your choices from 1 (most important) to 5 (least important). The ideas on this handout may help you get started.

Help make Christmas goodies.

Go to a special Christmas service.

Decorate the tree.

Wrap presents.

Visit a relative.

Buy presents.

Practice for the Christmas pageant or musical.

Make a list of what I want for Christmas.

Go Christmas caroling.

Go to a Christmas party.

Clean my room.

LESSON THREE

LESSON 3:
GOD'S SON IS BORN

the POINT  Jesus is God's Son.

■ ■ ■ ■ ■ ■ ■ ■ ■ ■ ■ ■ ■

BIBLE FOCUS

"For nothing is impossible with God" (Luke 1:37).

Hands-On
FUN
AT HOME

FUN food

Build an edible Nativity scene. Using marshmallow cream as glue, stick graham crackers together for the walls and roof of the stable. Make a manger for your stable by "gluing" toasted coconut to a graham cracker. Glue the graham cracker to four pretzel sticks for the manger's legs. You can shape warm Rice Krispies treat mixture into people for your Nativity scene. Be sure to put sandwich bags over your hands so the mixture doesn't stick to you! Your edible Nativity scene will be a treat to look at and to eat!

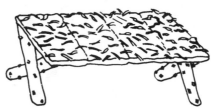

FAITH walk

Make a special place in your house to welcome Jesus this week. You might make a place in your room to pray or read your Bible. Or set an extra place at the dinner table and talk about what it might be like for Jesus to eat with your family. At the end of the week, talk about the special place(s) you made for Jesus. Did you think about Jesus more? Did you act differently? Are you glad you did this? Remember to welcome Jesus to your house every day!

CHECK it OUT

ETC.

Read John 1:12.
As a citizen of your country, you have certain rights. What rights do you have as a child of God?

Read John 3:16-17.
Why did God send Jesus into the world?

Talk with your family about what kinds of baby gifts you'd give Jesus if he were born today. Then get a small baby present and wrap it. Take your gift to a community agency, hospital, or church that could give your gift to a baby who needs it. Celebrate Jesus' birth by caring for another baby.

LESSON 4

WHAT ARE WE WAITING FOR?

THE POINT

God rewards those who trust him.

THE BIBLE BASIS

Luke 2:21-38. Simeon and Anna see Jesus.

The period immediately following Jesus' birth was a time to celebrate the rewards of trusting in God's promises. After months of waiting, Mary and Joseph had experienced the joy of Jesus' birth. Several weeks later, they took Jesus to the temple, where they met Simeon and Anna, who had waited for years to see their Savior. Simeon and Anna were thrilled but not surprised to discover that God had kept his promise to send his Son. The joy of seeing Jesus was worth the wait!

Third- and fourth-graders know the frustrations of waiting. They wait anxiously for Christmas, birthdays, and summer vacations. Some are waiting to be old enough to mow lawns or have baby-sitting jobs. Others are waiting to have their own rooms. This is a great time for kids to learn that waiting is part of life and to discover what things are worth waiting for. Use this lesson to teach your students that while they may sometimes have to wait, God is faithful and keeps his promises. And God rewards those who trust him.

Other Scriptures used in this lesson are **Philippians 4:6-7; Romans 8:27-28;** and **Isaiah 40:31.**

Students will

● explore the difficulty of waiting,

● understand that God's timing is worth waiting for, and

● discover ways to help them wait for God.

THIS LESSON AT A GLANCE

Before the lesson, collect the necessary items from the Learning Lab for the activities you plan to use. Refer to the pictures in the margin to see what each item looks like.

SECTION	MINUTES	WHAT STUDENTS WILL DO	LEARNING LAB SUPPLIES	CLASSROOM SUPPLIES
ATTENTION GRABBER	up to 10	**WE'RE WAITING!**—Name things that are hard to wait for.	Neon loops	
BIBLE EXPLORATION AND APPLICATION	up to 12	**DO YOU THINK YOU'LL LIVE TO SEE . . . ?**—Suggest future inventions and read Luke 2:21-35.	Neon loops, paper streamer roll, top pens, pine cones, cassette: "Inventor's Workshop"	Bibles, paper, pencils cassette player
	up to 12	**WHILE YOU WAIT**—Compare waiting quietly with doing something while they wait, and discuss Luke 2:36-38.	Shape puzzles	Bibles
	up to 15	**THE WAITING GAME**—Give advice about waiting based on Philippians 4:6-7; Romans 8:27-28; and Isaiah 40:31.		Bibles, "The Waiting Game" handouts (p. 57)
CLOSING	up to 11	**THE REWARD**—Give a treat as a reward and commit to trusting God.	Neon loops	Treats

Remember to make photocopies of the "Hands-On Fun at Home" handout (p. 58) to send home with your kids. The "Fun at Home" handout suggests ways for kids to talk with their families about what they're learning in class and helps them put their faith into action.

THE LESSON

As kids arrive, ask them which "Fun at Home" activities they tried. Ask questions such as "What special place in your home did you use to welcome Jesus?" and "What baby gifts did you and your family think Jesus would like if he were born today?"

Explain to the kids that whenever you ring the *gold foil bell,* they are to stop talking, raise their hands, and focus on you. Explain that it's important to respond to this signal quickly so the class can do as many fun activities as possible.

ATTENTION GRABBER

WE'RE WAITING!
(up to 10 minutes)

Form a circle and give each student a *neon loop.* Take two *neon loops* and show kids how to attach them to make a chain. Follow the margin illustrations to fold one loop over another, then pull the first loop through itself and pull it tight.

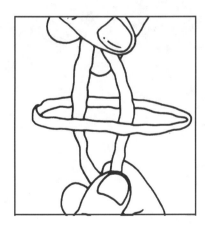

Say: **Think of something that's hard for you to wait for. For example, you might have a hard time waiting for Christmas or waiting for your turn in a game. Let's make a waiting chain. When it's your turn, name the thing that's hardest for you to wait for and add your loop to the chain. Then pass the chain to the person on your right. That person will repeat what you said and add something else that's hard to wait for. The next person will repeat what the first two people said and so on. I'll go first. It's hard for me to wait for our class to meet because I'm so excited to see all of you!**

If you have 10 or more students, break into two groups for this activity. Continue the activity until the chain reaches you again. Then bring everyone together and ask:

● **What thoughts went through your mind as you waited for the chain to come to you?** (I tried to think of something no one else had said; I was nervous that I wouldn't be able to remember what everyone had said.)

● **How was waiting for the chain like waiting for other things in life?** (Sometimes I get nervous waiting; it's hard to wait.)

● **What's it like to wait for good things, like Christmas?** (Sometimes I feel like it'll never come; it's hard to think about anything else.)

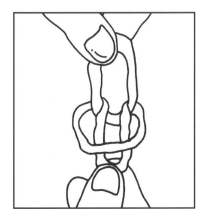

● **Why is Christmas worth waiting for?** (Because I get lots of presents; because I get to see all my cousins; because we celebrate Jesus' birth.)

Say: **We spend lots of time waiting. Usually the things that are hardest to wait for are the things we're really looking forward to.**

the POINT

Waiting takes patience, and we hope whatever we're waiting for will be worth it. Sometimes we have to wait for things to happen in God's time, even though we'd like to have them happen sooner! But we know the results will be worth the wait. ☞ **God rewards those who trust him.**

Dismantle the chain and return the loops to the kids. Say: **Hang your loop on one of your ears. You're going to need it later for something special. Trust me—it'll be worth it.**

LEARNING LAB

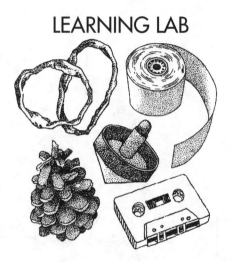

BIBLE EXPLORATION AND APPLICATION

DO YOU THINK YOU'LL LIVE TO SEE...?
(up to 12 minutes)

Set out the remaining *neon loops, paper streamer roll, top pens,* and *pine cones.* Form four groups and give each group a sheet of paper and a pencil. (A group may be one person.) Number the groups from 1 to 4. Ask:

● **What inventions do we use today that people years ago might not have been able to imagine?** (Car telephones; computers, VCRs; video games.)

Say: **Each group is now an "invention team." Your job is to think of new inventions you'd like to see in the future. Team 1, your job is to invent something that could be used in a doctor's office or a hospital. Team 2 will invent something that could be used in a school. Team 3 will invent something that could be used in a church. Team 4 will invent something that could be used at home. You may use any of the Learning Lab items I've set out to represent your invention, or just to spark your imagination. You'll have three minutes to come up with your ideas. Then we're going to guess what you invented.**

As kids are working, play the "Inventor's Workshop" segment of the *cassette tape.* After three minutes ring the *gold foil bell.* Wait for kids to respond, then say: **Now we'll see if the other groups can guess what your inventions are. I want each group to think of a way to act out your invention. For example, if you just invented the bicycle, one person could be the rider, two people could be the wheels, and one person could be the handlebars. You can pantomime the motion of your invention or link hands and form the shape of it. You'll also be allowed to give one clue. If you invented an automatic eraser, your clue might be, "Our invention will help you when you make a mistake." You'll have a few minutes to plan your presentations.**

After two or three minutes, ring the *gold foil bell* again. Have groups take turns presenting their inventions to the class. Have kids try to guess each invention as it's presented. If no one guesses, have the group describe its invention. After all the groups have presented their inventions, collect the Learning Lab items for use in future lessons. Ask:

● **How long do you think you'd have to wait for these things you created to actually be invented?** (I don't think it will ever happen; all my life; 50 years.)

Say: **People in Bible times had been waiting anxiously for the Savior to arrive. Let's read about one of those people now.** Distribute Bibles. Have kids look up **Luke 2:21-35.** Have a volunteer read the passage aloud as the rest of the kids follow along in their Bibles.

Ask:

● **What do you think it would be like to wait for something your whole life?** (Hard; exciting; frustrating.)

● **How do you think Simeon felt after he saw Jesus?** (Glad his long wait was over; excited; thankful.)

● **Have you ever waited and prayed a long time for something? Explain.** (I waited for my dad to get a job; I waited for my little sister to get well.)

● **What was it like when what you were waiting for finally happened?** (I was excited; I felt happy.)

Then say: **It's exciting to think about all the great inventions people will think of in the next 100 years. But it's even more exciting to watch for the wonderful things God will bring into our lives. Simeon spent his whole life waiting for God's Son, and he wasn't disappointed. The Holy Spirit told Simeon he wouldn't die before he saw Jesus, and that's just what happened. Simeon trusted God, and ✍ God rewards those who trust him.**

WHILE YOU WAIT
(up to 12 minutes)

Form two lines. Set one shape puzzle in front of each line. Say: **We're going to try to solve these *shape puzzles.* When it's your turn, you'll have 30 seconds to work on the puzzle. The rest of you will stand in line and quietly wait your turns. Don't talk or move around—we don't want to bother the people who are working on the puzzles. When you finish your turn, go to the end of the line and wait with the others.**

After all the kids have had a turn, ring the *gold foil bell* to regain their attention. Wait for kids to respond, then have them sit down in their lines. Ask:

● **What was it like to stand in line and wait quietly?** (Boring; not very fun.)

● **What thoughts went through your mind as you were waiting?** (I wished my turn would come soon; I hoped that our next activity would be more fun.)

 the POINT

LEARNING LAB

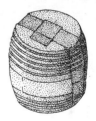

TEACHER TIP

If you have more than 12 students in your class, end the first round after three minutes.

Say: **We've already heard how Simeon waited to see Jesus. The book of Luke tells us about another person who was waiting for Jesus.** Distribute Bibles and have kids look up **Luke 2:36-38.** When everyone has found the passage, have a volunteer read it. Then ask:

● **What did Anna do while she waited for God to send Jesus?** (Worshiped God; prayed a lot; thanked God.)

● **Do you think the way she spent her time made waiting easier? Explain.** (Yes, because she could think about what she was waiting for; she got closer to God; she was prepared to see Jesus.)

Say: **Let's try our activity again, but this time I'll give you something to do while you're waiting for your turn at the puzzle.**

Switch the *shape puzzles* and have kids stand in their lines. Give one of the following directions to the lines each time someone new approaches the *shape puzzles.*

● **Give everyone high fives, jumping as high as you can.**

● **Shake hands with everyone and say, "God loves you!"**

● **Link elbows with another person. Walk around the room with that person as you both repeat, "I'm glad you're my friend."**

● **Tell two people about the last really good book you read.**

● **Ask the person behind you to pray for you or someone you know.**

After kids have completed the last instruction, call for their attention by ringing the *gold foil bell.* Collect the *shape puzzles* for use in future lessons. Ask:

● **What was it like to have something to do while you waited?** (Good; not as boring; I almost forgot I was waiting for something.)

● **How are the things you did while you waited to work on the** *shape puzzle* **like the things Anna did while she waited for God to send Jesus?** (Anna prayed a lot, and we listened to what other people wanted us to pray about; Anna was probably happy, and we had fun encouraging each other.)

● **What have you learned from this experience that could help you when you're waiting for God to work things out?** (I'll look for good things to do while I wait; I'll pray and read the Bible.)

Say: **We may not like to wait, but waiting can be a good thing! The story of Anna shows us that we don't have to just sit around as we wait—we can get to know God better, take positive action, and learn to trust. Then we'll find out for ourselves that** **God rewards those who trust him.**

 the POINT

THE WAITING GAME
(up to 15 minutes)

If you're running short on time, you may want to skip this activity and move on to the closing.

Form three groups. A group can be as small as one person. Distribute part 1 of "The Waiting Game" handout (p. 57) to each person in group 1.

LESSON FOUR

Distribute part 2 of the handout to the people in group 2 and part 3 to the people in group 3.

Say: **Choose one person in your group to read the first paragraph on your handout aloud. Another person can read the Scripture passage, then you can all discuss the questions together.**

After three minutes, ring the *gold foil bell*. Then say: **Form a trio with people from the other two groups. In your trios, take turns telling about the situation you discussed, the Scripture you read, and the advice you came up with.**

Allow about five minutes for kids to share in their trios. Then ring the *gold foil bell* to bring everyone together. Ask:

● **What's the best piece of advice you heard in your trio?** (To pray instead of worrying; to trust God to work things out for the best.)

● **What's one thing you learned from the Bible this morning that will help you when you face waiting situations in the future?** (That I can trust God to work things out; that God wants me to pray instead of worrying.)

Say: **It's great to know that**  **God rewards those who trust him. Some people may have to wait a lifetime, like Simeon and Anna did. Some wait a few months or weeks. But I can tell you this for sure: If you trust in God, you'll never be disappointed!**

We believe that Christian education extends beyond the classroom into the home. Photocopy the "Hands-On Fun at Home" handout (p. 58) for this week and send it home with your kids. Encourage kids to try several activities and discuss the Bible verses and questions with their parents.

CLOSING

THE REWARD
(up to 11 minutes)

Say: **Remember the *neon loops* I gave you at the beginning of the lesson? Let's see if they're still hanging on your ears. If they are, you're in luck because I have a treat for you.**

Distribute treats. Ask:

● **How did you feel when I asked you to wear the *neon loops* on your ears?** (Weird; a little embarrassed.)

● **Why did you go ahead and wear them?** (Because you told us to; because we trusted you when you said it would be worth it.)

● **How is the way you trusted me like the way God wants us to trust him?** (God wants us to trust him even if we have to wait a long

---

"For nothing is impossible with God" (Luke 1:37).

Kids often question whether God can do anything if he doesn't provide an immediate response to prayer. Remind them that God rewards those who trust his power and wisdom, and if they are patient, he will answer all their prayers.

✍ the POINT

LEARNING LAB

---

time for him to work things out; God wants us to trust him to keep his promises.)

Have kids form a circle.

the POINT

Say:  **God rewards those who trust him. Think back on all the things we talked about that are hard to wait for. Then single out one thing you're waiting for. When you've thought of it, toss your neon loop into the circle and say, "God, I trust you."**

When all the *neon loops* are in the center of the circle, close with a prayer similar to this one: **Lord, thank you for keeping your promise to Simeon and Anna. Thank you for caring about our concerns. We trust you and ask you to give us patience as you work things out. Help us to use our waiting time wisely. Amen.**

Collect the *neon loops* for use in later lessons.

Part 1

Jessica is the only child in her family. She's always wanted a little brother or sister. Jessica's parents decided to adopt a child, and now they're on a waiting list for a baby, but they don't know when they'll get one. Jessica thinks about the baby all the time. She wonders if it will be a boy or a girl, if it will cry a lot, and if she will be a good big sister.

Read Philippians 4:6-7.

● What advice could you give Jessica from these verses?

● What could Jessica do to make the waiting easier?

● What do you think Jessica might learn as she waits?

Part 2

Jim has played on the same park-district basketball team for two years. Last year his team ended up in second place. This year they have a good chance of winning the championship. Last Thursday Jim sprained his ankle in a scuffle for the ball. The doctor said it could take quite awhile to heal. Jim is worried about getting well in time for the playoffs.

Read Isaiah 40:31.

● What advice could you give Jim from these verses?

● What could Jim do to make the waiting easier?

● What do you think Jim might learn as he waits?

Part 3

The Clarksons live in a small apartment. Tony, who's in fourth grade, and Mikey, who just turned 3, have to share a bedroom. Tony is tired of Mikey getting into his stuff, and he's tired of tiptoeing around after Mikey goes to bed. The Clarksons have been saving money and looking for a house they can afford. Sometimes Tony feels like he'll never get a room of his own.

Read Romans 8:27-28.

● What advice could you give Tony from these verses?

● What could Tony do to make the waiting easier?

● What do you think Tony might learn as he waits?

Hands-On FUN!
AT HOME

the POINT ✍ God rewards those who trust him.

BIBLE FOCUS

"For nothing is impossible with God" (Luke 1:37).

CHECK it OUT

Read Isaiah 40:31.
Name one way God could help you when you're tired of waiting.

Read I Corinthians 13:7.
Name one area of your life in which you'd like to be more patient.

Read Hebrews 6:12.
What's one good thing you could do while you wait?

WAY to PRAY

Ask your parents to purchase a blank book to use as a family prayer log. Once a week or once a month, sit down together and record your prayer concerns. Write prayer concerns on one page and keep the facing page blank for writing God's answers to your prayers. You'll be excited as you fill up the answer pages and discover how God is working in your lives!

FAITH walk

Remember taking a family trip and asking your parents over and over, "When are we going to get there?" Turn the tables and take your parents on a trip. You might lead them on a walk or a bike ride. Choose a place you think they'd like to go, but don't tell them exactly where you're going. Count how many times they ask you where they're going or when they'll get there. When you arrive at your destination, talk about whether it was hard for them to be patient. Give them a big hug and a treat for being good travelers.

SWEET treats

Ask a parent to help you make a sweet treat for your family. Follow the recipe to make delicious Honey Cookies. While you're waiting for the cookies to bake in the oven, talk about how sometimes God asks us to wait, too. Just as we have to wait for yummy cookies to bake before we can enjoy them, we may have to wait for the good things God has planned for us.

Honey Cookies
½ cup honey
½ cup packed brown sugar
½ cup softened butter
1 egg
1½ cups flour
¼ teaspoon salt
½ teaspoon baking soda
¼ teaspoon cinnamon
¼ teaspoon nutmeg
1. Preheat oven to 350 degrees.
2. Mix ingredients in order.
3. Drop by spoonfuls onto un-greased cookie sheet.
4. Bake until lightly browned.

LESSON 5

READY, SET, GROW!

THE POINT

☞ God wants us to learn and grow.

THE BIBLE BASIS

Luke 2:41-52. Jesus asks questions in the temple.

The gospels are full of amazing stories about Jesus' birth and adulthood, but they tell only one story about Jesus' childhood. This passage about Jesus speaking with the temple priests demonstrates that Jesus was both a human boy and the Son of God. He learned, asked questions, and grew mentally and physically, just like other children. But he was also divine. Even at the age of 12, Jesus was aware that he needed to be involved in God's work in the world.

At school, kids learn important social skills as well as math, spelling, and other subjects. Kids know that the purpose of going to school is to learn, but they may not think of church as a place to learn, to stretch their minds, and to grow. Use this lesson to teach kids that they can ask questions and learn more about God at church—and that what they learn at church can have a powerful, positive impact on their daily lives. By looking at the example of Jesus' boyhood, your students will learn that God wants each of them to learn and grow.

Other Scriptures used in this lesson are **Matthew 5:13-15, 43-48; 6:25-27.**

GETTING THE POINT

Students will
- learn the importance of asking questions,
- discover that church is a place to learn, and
- understand that they can always learn more about God.

THIS LESSON AT A GLANCE

Before the lesson, collect the necessary items from the Learning Lab for the activities you plan to use. Refer to the pictures in the margin to see what each item looks like.

SECTION	MINUTES	WHAT STUDENTS WILL DO	LEARNING LAB SUPPLIES	CLASSROOM SUPPLIES
ATTENTION GRABBER	up to 10	**DON'T ASK ME**—Try to find answers without asking questions.		Pencils, paper, chalkboard and chalk or newsprint and a marker
BIBLE EXPLORATION AND APPLICATION	up to 12	**WHAT DO YOU WANT TO KNOW?**—List questions they might ask about God and read Luke 2:41-46.	Paper streamer roll	Bibles, pencils
	up to 12	**TOP-PEN QUESTION SPIN**—Demonstrate what they've learned and read Luke 2:47-50.	Top pens, cassette: "Game Show"	Bibles, "Top-Pen Question Spin" handout (p. 66), scissors, cassette player
	up to 15	**SUPER STUDENTS**—Develop questions based on various Scriptures in Matthew.		Bibles, pencils, paper
CLOSING	up to 11	**GROW FOR IT!**—Read Luke 2:51-52 and make spiritual growth charts.	Paper streamer roll	Bibles, scissors, marker, newsprint, pencils, tape

Remember to make photocopies of the "Hands-On Fun at Home" handout (p. 67) to send home with your kids. The "Fun at Home" handout suggests ways for kids to talk with their families about what they're learning in class and helps them put their faith into action.

THE LESSON

As kids arrive, ask them which "Fun at Home" activities they tried. Ask questions such as "What was it like to share prayer concerns in your family log book?" and "How did your family handle their impatience on your pretend trip?"

Tell kids that whenever you ring the *gold foil bell,* they are to stop talking, raise their hands, and focus on you. Explain that it's important to respond to this signal quickly so the class can do as many fun activities as possible.

MODULE REVIEW

KEY VERSE
CONNECTION

"For nothing is impossible with God" (Luke 1:37).

Knowing the power of God comes through discovering him. Use the Key Verse to teach your kids that learning about God and growing with God will help them understand how God can do anything.

Use the casual interaction time at the beginning of class to ask kids the following module-review questions.

● **Did you have to wait for anything this week? What did you do or think about as you waited?**

● **What have you done to make room for Jesus in your life?**

● **What are some ways God has used you in the past few weeks?**

● **What "impossible" things has God helped you do this month?**

● **How is your life different as a result of what we've learned in class this month?**

Before class, write the following instructions on a chalkboard or newsprint.

● Find out where three people were born.

● Find out two people's favorite color.

● Find out one person's favorite sport or activity.

Adapt your instructions to fit your class. For example, if everyone in your class was born in the same town, you might request other information such as middle names or birthdays.

ATTENTION GRABBER

DON'T ASK ME
(up to 10 minutes)

Distribute pencils and paper. Point to the instructions you've written on the chalkboard or newsprint and say: **You'll have three minutes to get this information from your classmates. However, there is one rule in this game. You can't ask any questions. If you ask a question, you'll be disqualified. You can find information any other way.**

the POINT

LEARNING LAB

the POINT

After three minutes, ring the *gold foil bell*. Read each instruction and have kids share any information they were able to gather. Applaud everyone's efforts, then ask:

● **What was it like to want to know something when you couldn't ask questions to find the answers?** (Frustrating; I felt dumb; it made me mad.)

● **Do you think it's possible to learn without asking questions? Why or why not?** (Yes, sometimes we learn by looking at things, like in science; we learn the things our teachers tell us whether we ask questions or not.)

● **Do you think God wants us to ask questions? Explain.** (Yes, because God wants us to learn more; no, God just wants us to believe in him.)

Say: **It's hard to learn without asking questions. We have lots to learn about God and about what we believe. And the best way to learn about those things is to ask!** **God wants us to learn and grow. We're going to practice some ways to do that today.**

BIBLE EXPLORATION AND APPLICATION

WHAT DO YOU WANT TO KNOW?
(up to 12 minutes)

Form pairs and distribute Bibles. Give each pair a pencil and a strip of paper from the *paper streamer roll*.

Say: **The Bible tells us that when Jesus was not much older than you, he was busy asking questions about God. Let's find out more. Read Luke 2:41-46. Then take two or three minutes to make a list of all the questions you'd like to ask your church teachers or leaders about God.**

Ring the *gold foil bell* after two or three minutes. Have pairs take turns sharing their questions with the class. Congratulate kids on their good thinking, then ask:

● **Why do you think Luke wrote about Jesus asking questions at the temple?** (Because he was writing about Jesus' life; to show us that asking questions is good; to teach us that learning about God is part of growing up.)

● **What is it like to ask questions at church?** (Sometimes I'm afraid that if I ask a question, people will think it's dumb; I feel good because I know the teachers can help me find the answers.)

Say: **Your teachers and leaders at church are here to encourage you to grow up to be the person God wants you to be. Just as Jesus listened and asked questions at the temple, we hope you'll listen and ask questions at church because** **God wants us to learn and grow.**

LESSON FIVE

TOP-PEN QUESTION SPIN
(up to 12 minutes)

Before class, cut apart the questions on the "Top-Pen Question Spin" handout (p. 66). Put the question slips for round 1 in the lid of the Learning Lab or in another container. Set the question slips for round 2 aside until needed.

Help kids form up to four groups. Have each group choose a representative to draw the questions out of the box, a spinner to spin the *top pen,* and a reader to read the Scripture passage.

Say: **The people who heard Jesus in the temple were amazed at how much he knew at such a young age. Even his parents were amazed.** Have groups read **Luke 2:47-50.** Say: **Today we're going to play a game that will give you a chance to demonstrate your knowledge of lots of different things. Welcome to "Top-Pen Question Spin!"**

Play the "Game Show" segment of the *cassette tape.* As the music plays, hand the spinner in each group a *top pen.* Have the representative from each team step forward. Say: **We'll play two rounds of this game. When it's your team's turn, each of you will draw a question for your team. As soon as you read your question aloud, the spinner should spin your team's *top pen.* Your team may keep giving answers to your question as long as the top is spinning. Each person must give an answer before anyone answers twice. Only one person may talk at a time. Your team will earn 1 point for each answer.**

After each team has taken a turn, ring the *gold foil bell* to signal the end of round 1. Remove the round 1 question slips and replace them with the question slips for round 2. Play the second round.

After the second round, total the scores and applaud the winning team. Collect the *top pens* for use in future lessons. Ask:

● **What did you think as you tried to name all the things you've learned at church?** (I was surprised there were so many; I felt smart; I felt older.)

● **How did you learn all those things?** (From teachers; by listening and remembering; by studying; by asking questions.)

● **What have you learned at church that has made a difference in your life?** (To love other people; to share what I have with others; not to tell lies.)

Say: God wants us to learn and grow. We come to church to learn about God and the way God wants us to live. God created us with bright minds, and he wants us to make the most of them. We can use our minds at church to think and ask questions that will help us put what we've learned into practice.

TEACHER TIP

If you have a small class, form two or three groups or assign kids more than one role.

TEACHER TIP

To make scoring easier, you'll want to have easy access to some answers. The Ten Commandments are found in Exodus 20, and you'll find the names of the 12 disciples in Matthew 10:1-4.

 the POINT

Have kids number off by threes. Have the 1s, 2s, and 3s gather in separate areas of the room. Give each group paper, a pencil, and Bibles. Say: **When Jesus grew up, he traveled around the country teaching people how God wanted them to live. Many of Jesus' teachings are recorded in the New Testament. We're going to see what we can learn from Jesus' teachings today.**

Assign each group one of the following Scripture passages: **Matthew 5:13-15; Matthew 5:43-48; Matthew 6:25-27.**

Say: **Choose one person to read aloud the Scripture I've assigned to your group. Discuss the passage with your group and write down one or two questions you have about it.**

After about five minutes, ring the *gold foil bell* to bring everyone together.

Invite kids from each group to summarize their Scripture and share their questions. Challenge kids to respond to one another's questions.

Wrap up the discussion by asking:

● **What was it like to come up with your own questions about the Bible?** (Hard—I didn't know what to ask; easy, because there were lots of things I didn't understand about my passage.)

● **Do you think that making up your own questions helped you learn? Why or why not?** (Yes, because I had to think about it more; asking questions helped me understand better; no, it just made me more confused.)

Say:  **God wants us to learn and grow, and asking questions is one way we can do that. This week's "Hands-On Fun at Home" paper will provide you with more questions to work on at home. Talk about your questions with your family and other people you know. God wants them to learn and grow, too!**

TEACHER TIP

Circulate among the three areas as kids are working. If kids need help coming up with questions, offer them examples such as "What does it mean to be a light of the world?" **(Matthew 5:13-15)**, "What should I say when I pray for my enemies" **(Matthew 5:43-48)**, or "How can I keep from worrying?" **(Matthew 6:25-27)**.

the POINT ☞

Hands-On FUN AT HOME

We believe that Christian education extends beyond the classroom into the home. Photocopy the "Hands-On Fun at Home" handout (p. 67) for this week and send it home with your kids. Encourage kids to try several activities and discuss the Bible verses and questions with their parents.

✍ the POINT

GROW FOR IT!
(up to 11 minutes)

Say: **Jesus continued to learn and grow, and that pleased God. Let's read about that right now.** Have kids look up **Luke 2:51-52** in their Bibles. After everyone has found the passage, ask a volunteer to read it to the class.

Say: ☞ **God wants us to learn and grow, just like Jesus did when he was a boy. Let's think of ways we can learn and grow in our faith during the next few weeks.**

Have kids share ways they'd like to grow in their faith. List their responses on a sheet of newsprint taped to a wall. If kids are slow to respond, offer suggestions such as being patient with younger siblings, inviting friends to church, or reading the Bible more often.

After you've compiled your list, distribute pencils and 2-foot lengths of *paper streamer roll.* Say: **Using the suggestions we've listed on the newsprint, make a spiritual growth chart for yourself. Make four marks on your streamer, one for each week, and label each mark with one way you want to grow in your faith during the next month.**

Give kids about five minutes to complete their spiritual growth charts. Then call for their attention by ringing the *gold foil bell.* Wait for kids to respond, then gather everyone in a circle. Have kids touch hands in the center of the circle. Say: **Let's each share one way we want to grow in our faith. After someone shares, we'll say that person's name three times and shout, "Grow for it!"**

Close by leading a prayer similar to this one: **Dear God, we have lots of questions and things to learn. Help us learn and grow like Jesus did. Amen.**

BIBLE *INSIGHT*

Luke did not portray Jesus as developing unusual powers, nor did he see Jesus' growth in wisdom as a detraction from his deity. Instead he emphasized that Jesus was willing to give up his place with God to develop normally and become a man (see Philippians 2:7).

TOP-PEN QUESTION SPIN

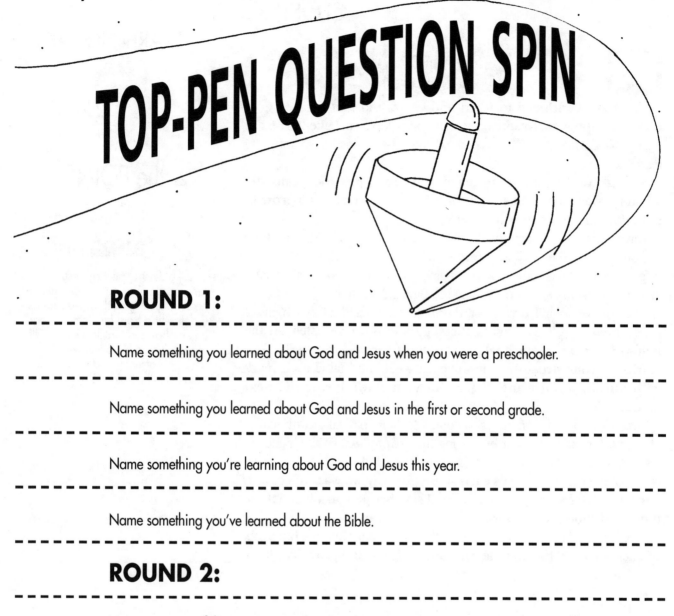

ROUND 1:

Name something you learned about God and Jesus when you were a preschooler.

Name something you learned about God and Jesus in the first or second grade.

Name something you're learning about God and Jesus this year.

Name something you've learned about the Bible.

ROUND 2:

Name as many of the Ten Commandments as you can.

Name as many of Jesus' miracles as you can.

Name as many of Jesus' 12 disciples as you can.

Name as many books of the Bible as you can.

LESSON FIVE

LESSON 5:
READY, SET, GROW!

the POINT ☞ **God wants us to learn and grow.**

■ ■ ■ ■ ■ ■ ■ ■ ■ ■ ■ ■ ■ ■

BIBLE FOCUS

"For nothing is impossible with God"
(Luke 1:37).

Start

Follow the steps in the know-and-grow trail to learn more about God and to grow in your faith this week.

Read a newspaper article that describes a problem in your town or country. Talk with your family about what Jesus might do in that situation.

Make a note of something you learned at school this week that might help you grow in your faith. It might be something you learned in class, on the playground, or something you learned about yourself.

Read from three books of the Bible you've never read before.

KNOW AND GROW

Do something kind for someone today. Afterward, think about what you learned from what you did.

Write one question about God you'll work on answering this month. Keep notes of your thoughts about this question. At the end of the month, ask a parent, teacher, or another adult the question, then compare your answers.

Pray about inviting someone to church. If God brings someone to mind, ask that person to go with you.

Write down one way you've grown in your faith this week.

finish!

Gather your family members together and have them each share one way they'd like to grow in faith. Brainstorm ways you can help one another, then pray for God's help as you all grow in faith.

JESUS' MIRACLES

■ ■ ■ ■ ■ ■ ■ ■ ■ ■ ■ ■ ■

Nothing captures kids' attention like the supernatural. Third- and fourth-graders spend much of their free time watching TV programs about superheroes or playing with superhero toys or video games. Kids may feel helpless in a world controlled by adults. But kids feel powerful and in control when watching and imitating the superheroes in their favorite TV programs.

But who has the real power? Third- and fourth-graders are ready to distinguish fantasy from reality. One of the greatest gifts you can give your kids is the knowledge that the God who created the universe, who lived and died as a man and rose again—that same God loves them and watches over them. These four lessons will teach kids that Jesus has more power than any superhero, and he can put his power to work in their lives.

JESUS' MIRACLES

LESSON	PAGE	THE POINT	THE BIBLE BASIS
6—OUR MIRACULOUS GOD	73	Jesus performed miracles so people would believe in God.	John 2:1-11
7—OUR HEALING GOD	83	Jesus is able to take care of our hurts.	Luke 5:17-26
8—TAPPING INTO GOD'S POWER	93	Jesus' power comes from God.	Luke 9:28-36
9—DOWN WITH DEATH!	103	Jesus has power over death.	John 11:1-44

THE SIGNAL

LEARNING LAB

During the lessons on miracles, your signal to get kids back together will be ringing the *gold foil bell* found in the Learning Lab. In response to your ringing the bell, kids will immediately stop talking, raise their hands, and focus their attention on you. Tell kids about this signal before starting each lesson. Explain that it's important to respond to the signal quickly so the class can do as many fun activities as possible.

During the lessons, you'll be prompted when to use the signal.

LEARNING LAB

THE TIME STUFFER

The Time Stuffer for the lessons on Jesus' miracles is the "I Spy a Miracle" poster found in the Learning Lab. During their free moments, kids can go to the poster, find miracles from the Bible and from nature, and identify them on the poster. By the end of the module, your students will have identified many miraculous things God has done for his people.

REMEMBERING THE BIBLE

Each four- or five-week module focuses on a key Bible verse. The key verse for this module is " 'I am the way and the truth and the life. No one comes to the Father except through me' " (John 14:6).

Following are two activities you may do with your third- and fourth-graders to help them remember this Bible verse and apply it to their lives.

LEARNING LAB

ONE WAY

Before class, hide a bag of treats somewhere in the church. Mark a trail leading to the treats with the *Indian corn*. Mark false trails with the *neon loops* and the *multicolored feathers*. If possible, make the *Indian corn* trail longer and more difficult than the other two. It could lead up and down stairs or under tables or pews. Post signs at the end of the false trails with messages such as "Sorry!" or "Wrong Way." Print the key verse on a blackboard or newsprint in the classroom.

As kids arrive, say: **One of these trails leads to a great reward. If you choose the right trail, you'll get to share the reward. Once you select a trail, you must follow it to the end.**

Let kids pick a trail and follow it. Have the kids who chose the *Indian corn* trail bring the treats back to the room. After all the kids have returned, ask:

● **How did you know which trail to follow?** (I just guessed; I went with my friends.)

● **What was your reaction when you reached the end of your trail?** (I was happy I got the reward; I was disappointed; I felt cheated.)

Lead kids in repeating the key verse together. Ask:

● **How is choosing the right trail like deciding to follow Jesus?** (There was only one right trail to the reward, and Jesus is the only way to get to God; if we follow Jesus we'll be rewarded in the end.)

To close, have kids form pairs and tell each other one way they'll follow Jesus this week. Then have them form a circle, join hands, and repeat the verse together.

WAY, TRUTH, AND LIFE RAP

Write the key verse on a sheet of newsprint and post it on a wall. Lead kids in reading the verse together, then form trios and have kids make up motions to go with the verse. For example, kids might point straight ahead to indicate "the way," raise their right hands to indicate "the truth," and sprout up like a plant to indicate "the life." Encourage kids to put rhythms with their motions as well.

After about five minutes, have trios present their motions to the class. Have the whole class agree on a set of motions to learn and present to parents at a later time.

JESUS' MIRACLES

LESSON 6

OUR MIRACULOUS GOD

THE POINT

☞ Jesus performed miracles so people would believe in God.

THE BIBLE BASIS

John 2:1-11. Jesus turns water to wine.

It may have begun as an ordinary day. Jesus, his followers, and his mother had been invited to a wedding. While they were enjoying the festivities, a problem arose—the host ran out of wine. At that point, an ordinary day turned extraordinary as Jesus performed the miracle that would begin his ministry. When Jesus turned the water into wine that day, many followers were convinced he truly was the Son of God.

Third- and fourth-graders are beginning to question things they see and hear. With their growing knowledge of science, they may doubt that miracles can happen today. But Jesus is as concerned about the details of your students' lives as he was about the wine at the wedding. Use this lesson to teach your students that Jesus is intimately, miraculously involved in our world and in their lives.

Other Scriptures used in this lesson are **Psalm 8; Mark 2:1-12; 4:35-41; Luke 8:40-42, 49-56; 18:35-43;** and **John 6:1-14.**

OUR MIRACULOUS GOD

73

GETTING THE POINT

Students will
- learn what miracles are,
- understand the difference between miracles and "magic," and
- recognize God's miraculous power.

THIS LESSON AT A GLANCE

Before the lesson, collect the necessary items from the Learning Lab for the activities you plan to use. Refer to the pictures in the margin to see what each item looks like.

SECTION	MINUTES	WHAT STUDENTS WILL DO	LEARNING LAB SUPPLIES	CLASSROOM SUPPLIES
ATTENTION GRABBER	up to 10	**"MAGIC" OR MIRACLE?**—See through a magic trick and compare it with a miracle.	Accordion flower	
BIBLE EXPLORATION AND APPLICATION	up to 12	**MIRACLE PUNCH**—Read John 2:1-11 and see the difference between modern conveniences and miracles.		Bibles, cups, pitcher of water, spoon, pre-sweetened drink mix
	up to 12	**SHARE-A-SNACK**—Share a doughnut and discuss John 6:1-14.		Bibles, doughnut, newsprint and marker or chalkboard and chalk
	up to 20	**ASTOUNDING!**—Read various Scriptures from Mark and Luke and write headlines and news reports about Bible miracles.		Bibles, "Astounding!" handouts (p. 80), pencils
CLOSING	up to 6	**IT'S A MIRACLE!**—Praise God for everyday miracles in nature and in their lives.	Pine cone, cassette: "It's a Miracle," "Lyrics Poster"	Bibles, cassette player

Remember to make photocopies of the "Hands-On Fun at Home" handout (p. 81) to send home with your kids. The "Fun at Home" handout suggests ways for kids to talk with their families about what they're learning in class and helps them put their faith into action.

THE LESSON

As kids arrive, ask them which "Fun at Home" activities they tried. Ask questions such as "What was one way you grew in faith last week?" and "Which books of the Bible did you read from during the past week?"

Tell kids that whenever you ring the *gold foil bell,* they are to stop talking, raise their hands, and focus on you. Explain that it's important to respond to this signal quickly so the class can do as many fun activities as possible. Practice the signal two or three times.

ATTENTION GRABBER

"MAGIC" OR MIRACLE?
(up to 10 minutes)

Say: **I'm going to show you an object that you've probably never seen before. After I show it to you, tell me what the object is like. What colors do you see? What does the object remind you of?**

Stretch out the *accordion flower* so kids can see only the accordionlike top. Have several volunteers share their observations with the class. Then have kids watch as you rotate the *accordion flower* into a circle and tap its base against your finger to open it completely. Ask:

● **Where did all the flowers come from?** (I don't know; from underneath.)

● **Do you think I produced these flowers by doing some kind of trick? Why or why not?** (Sort of, because they just appeared; no, they were hidden underneath all along; I don't know.)

● **Do you think I produced these flowers by a miracle? Why or why not?** (No, only God can do miracles; miracles are more exciting than a paper flower.)

Show kids how the folds of the *accordion flower* tuck under each other to hide the different parts. Pass the *accordion flower* around so kids can examine it for themselves. Ask:

● **What's the difference between miracles and magic tricks?** (Only God can do miracles; miracles are real, but magic is just a trick.)

Say: **After I showed you how the flower worked, you realized it wasn't magic. What people call "magic" is usually just a trick. Anyone can learn to do a trick. Miracles, on the other hand, rely on God's power. Miracles don't use tricks, and they can't be explained away.** ☞**Jesus performed miracles so people would believe in God. Let's learn about one of Jesus' miracles right now.**

Retrieve the *accordion flower* for use in future lessons.

TEACHER TIP

You may want to practice with the *accordion flower* before class. Bring the two bars together. Then tap the bars against your finger until the flower opens up. It may take a few tries.

 the POINT

BIBLE EXPLORATION AND APPLICATION

MIRACLE PUNCH
(up to 12 minutes)

Set out cups, pre-sweetened drink mix, a spoon, and a pitcher of water. Say: **Right now we're going to hear about a miracle Jesus performed.** Distribute Bibles and have kids look up **John 2:1-11.** Have a volunteer read the passage aloud as other kids follow along in their Bibles. Have another volunteer summarize the passage.

Then hold up the drink mix and say: **To help us remember this Bible story, I'm going to perform a fabulous miracle. Using only the supplies you see on this table, I will turn this water into punch. Stand up if you think I can perform this miracle.**

Wait for kids to stand, then motion for them to sit down again. Stir the drink mix into the water and hold up the pitcher. Say: **Stand up if you think my miracle was successful.**

Wait for kids to stand, then take a bow. Say: **Sit down if you'd like to sample my miraculous creation. Applaud loudly if you think I should become a professional miracle worker.**

Distribute drinks to the kids. Ask:

● **Did I turn this water into punch by my miraculous power? Explain.** (No, it was turned into punch by the drink mix; the only power you used was to stir it up.)

● **What's the difference between Jesus turning the water into wine and my turning the water into punch?** (Jesus did a miracle, but you just used a drink mix to make punch; Jesus did something impossible, but you did something easy.)

Say: **Any chemist could explain exactly what happened when I turned the water into punch. But when Jesus turned the water into wine, he caused an unexplainable, miraculous event to occur.** 📝 **Jesus performed miracles so people would believe in God.**

the POINT 📝

SHARE-A-SNACK
(up to 12 minutes)

Say: **It would be nice to have something to eat with our punch. I brought a snack—my favorite kind of doughnut.** Hold up the doughnut. **This doughnut is so good, I want to share it with all of you.**

Pinch off a small piece of doughnut for each student. Say: **Check it out! I made this one doughnut feed the whole class. Now you must really be impressed with my miraculous powers!** Ask:

● **Do you think the way I divided the doughnut was a miracle? Why or why not?** (No, all you did was break off little pieces.)

Say: **You kids are hard to please! First I turned water into punch, then I made one doughnut feed the whole class. And you're still not impressed. Well, I have to admit that there's nothing spectacular about making punch or breaking a doughnut into crumbs. I'm really not in the miracle business. But Jesus is! Let's look at another miracle Jesus performed.**

Form pairs. Distribute Bibles and have kids read **John 6:1-14.** Have partners alternate reading and summarizing the verses. While kids are reading, write the following questions on a chalkboard or newsprint. Have partners discuss each question.

● **Do you think the way Jesus divided the bread and fish was a miracle? Why or why not?** (Yes, because he couldn't have broken a loaf of bread into a thousand pieces; he had so much left over that it had to be a miracle.)

● **How do you think the people felt when they saw that huge crowd being fed with just five loaves and two fish?** (Amazed; they couldn't believe it; curious about how Jesus could do it.)

● **Jesus could have sent the people home to find food. Why do you think he fed them instead?** (Because he didn't want them to go hungry; to show them how powerful he was.)

After a few minutes, ring the *gold foil bell.* Wait for kids to respond, then invite partners to share their responses to the questions.

After all the kids have shared their answers, say: **Jesus fed all those people because he cared about their needs. He never performed miracles just to amaze people with his great power.** 🖎 **Jesus performed miracles so people would believe in God.**

ASTOUNDING!
(up to 20 minutes)

Before class, make photocopies of the "Astounding!" handout (p. 80). Form groups of no more than four and distribute Bibles and pencils. Have each group select a reader to read the Bible passage, a recorder to write down the story's details, and two reporters to "broadcast" the story. Write the following Scripture references on small slips of paper: **Mark 2:1-12; Mark 4:35-41; Luke 8:40-42, 49-56;** and **Luke 18:35-43.** Give each group a Scripture reference.

Say: **Pretend you're living in Bible times. You're just average citizens, and you've heard about Jesus and his amazing miracles. You've been asked to follow Jesus around for a while and write a story for the local newspaper about one of his miracles. Work together in your group to create a headline and news report for the story you've been assigned. You'll have about five minutes to create your stories.**

Give each group a copy of the "Astounding!" handout. Circulate among the groups to answer questions and contribute ideas.

After five minutes, ring the *gold foil bell.* Wait for kids to respond, then

the POINT

have reporters present their headlines and stories. After all the stories have been presented, ask:

● **Do you think people in Jesus' time would believe astounding headlines like the ones you wrote? Why or why not?** (Yes, because the events really happened; not unless they actually saw the miracle.)

● **Do you think people today would believe your stories? Why or why not?** (No, because the headlines sound too much like the National Enquirer; yes, but only if they knew about Jesus.)

the POINT

Say: **Jesus performed many amazing miracles. But, unlike the stories we sometimes read in newspapers today, Jesus' miracles really happened. When people saw the wonderful and amazing things Jesus did, they knew he was God's Son.**  **Jesus performed miracles so people would believe in God.**

 We believe that Christian education extends beyond the classroom into the home. Photocopy the "Hands-On Fun at Home" handout (p. 81) for this week and send it home with your kids. Encourage kids to try several activities and discuss the Bible verses and questions with their parents.

LEARNING LAB

CLOSING

IT'S A MIRACLE!
(up to 6 minutes)

Distribute Bibles. Say: **Let's think about miracles we can see every day.** Have kids look up **Psalm 8** and read it with a partner.

Hold up a *pine cone* from the Learning Lab. Say: **In addition to the miracles Jesus performed, we see God's miracles every day in nature. Pine trees make hard cones to protect their seeds. Rainbows appear after it rains. Each snowflake is different. We're going to learn a song now that celebrates God's "everyday" miracles.**

Lead kids in singing "It's a Miracle" with the *cassette tape*. Use the "Lyrics Poster" found in the Learning Lab to assist you.

Form a circle and have kids join hands. Say: **Using a miracle from the song we just learned or another "everyday" miracle you know of, complete the sentence: I believe in God because of... For example, you might say, "I believe in God because of rainbows," or "I believe in God because of birds' nests." As you complete the sentence, raise your right hand. We'll go around the circle until we've all raised our hands. Then we'll say together, "I believe in you, God" as we drop our hands.**

After you drop your hands, say:  **Jesus performed miracles so people would believe in God. Our God has created many wonderful and miraculous things for us to enjoy. He's also created each one of us in a special, miraculous way. Our eyes see, our ears hear, and our arms and legs move. We are all God's miracles. Let's thank God for that now.**

Close in prayer, thanking God for the miracle of each student's life.

Astounding!
Headline

_____

_____

Who was there: _____

What happened: _____

_____

_____

_____

_____

_____

_____

_____

_____

_____

_____

_____

_____

_____

_____

LESSON 6:
OUR MIRACULOUS GOD

the POINT ☞ **Jesus performed miracles so people would believe in God.**

BIBLE FOCUS

"Jesus answered, 'I am the way and the truth and the life. No one comes to the Father except through me' " (John 14:6).

UNLOCK the DOOR

Jesus said in John 14:6, "No one comes to the Father except through me." Make a cardboard key like the one below and write "Jesus is the key to heaven" on it. Punch a hole in the top of the key and thread a piece of yarn through it. Wear the key as a necklace or hang it from a doorknob to remind you of the miracle of Jesus' love.

"Jesus is the key to heaven."

WAY to PRAY

Read Psalm 77:11-14 together. Then take turns remembering God's miracles and celebrating them. Say, "I remember the miracles you did for..." Fill in the blank with your favorite Bible character such as Moses or David. Then thank God for the little miracles he's done for your family or others you know. Use the same sentence prayer but fill in the name of the person you know and tell what God has done for him or her.

CHECK it OUT

Read John 5:36.
Was it easier for people who saw Jesus' miracles to believe he was God's Son, or is it easier for people today who read about his miracles in the Bible? Explain.

Read Acts 8:5-25.
What was the difference between the miracles Simon the sorcerer did and the miracles Philip did?

Read Job 38:1-35.
Take a short walk. What miracles of nature can you see right in your own neighborhood?

FAITH walk

Read about faith as big as a mustard seed in Matthew 17:14-20. Buy a packet of mustard seeds at a garden shop. At dinner one evening, pass around the seeds so everyone can see how small they are. Plant a few seeds in a pot or in your back yard. Each time you water the plant, pray that your faith will keep growing, too.

LESSON 7

OUR HEALING GOD

"Jesus answered, 'I am the way and the truth and the life. No one comes to the Father except through me' "

(John 14:6).

THE POINT

Jesus is able to take care of our hurts.

THE BIBLE BASIS

Luke 5:17-26. Jesus heals a paralyzed man.

News spread quickly about Jesus' healing power. Soon people from all around the region were bringing their sick friends and family members to Jesus to be healed. Those who carried the paralyzed man to Jesus overcame many obstacles in the process. They hoisted the man to the roof; they dug a hole through several layers of clay, reeds, grass, and branches; then they lowered the man through the hole in the ceiling, into the crowd before Jesus. After expending all that effort, they may have been confused when Jesus spoke of spiritual rather than physical healing. Yet by healing the man's spirit as well as his body, Jesus demonstrated that he was more than just a miracle worker—he was the Son of God.

Third- and fourth-graders today experience a multitude of physical, spiritual, and emotional hurts. They get knocked down physically and verbally on the school ground; they worry when parents argue; they hurt when friends betray their trust. Third- and fourth-graders are also discovering that sinful actions produce hurtful consequences. Use this lesson to teach kids that Jesus is able to heal of their hurts, including the hurt of sin.

Other Scriptures used in this lesson are **Romans 6:23** and **2 Corinthians 1:3-5.**

OUR HEALING GOD

GETTING THE POINT

Students will
- identify "outside" and "inside" hurts they've experienced,
- discuss positive ways to handle their hurts, and
- understand that sin is a hurt that needs to be healed.

THIS LESSON AT A GLANCE

Before the lesson, collect the necessary items from the Learning Lab for the activities you plan to use. Refer to the pictures in the margin to see what each item looks like.

SECTION	MINUTES	WHAT STUDENTS WILL DO	LEARNING LAB SUPPLIES	CLASSROOM SUPPLIES
ATTENTION GRABBER	up to 10	**STUCK IN THE MUD**—Think about what it's like to be paralyzed by imagining they're stuck in a mud pit.		
BIBLE EXPLORATION AND APPLICATION	up to 15	**I HATE IT WHEN THAT HAPPENS . . .**—Decide how to handle their hurts and read 2 Corinthians 1:3-5.	Cassette: "That Really Hurts"	Bibles, cassette player, markers, newsprint, tape, blackboard, chalk
	up to 15	**CARRIED AWAY**—Read Luke 5:17-26 and carry each other across the room.		Bibles, blackboard, chalk
	up to 15	**FREE!**—Read Romans 6:23 and discuss how Jesus can free them from the hurt of sin.	Metallic ribbons, paper streamer roll	Bible, scissors, newsprint, marker, pencils, tape, wastebasket
CLOSING	up to 5	**BAND-AID PRAYERS**—Commit to praying for each other's hurts.		Adhesive bandages

Remember to make photocopies of the "Hands-On Fun at Home" handout (p. 91) to send home with your kids. The "Fun at Home" handout suggests ways for kids to talk with their families about what they're learning in class and helps them put their faith into action.

THE LESSON

As kids arrive, ask them which "Fun at Home" activities they tried. Ask questions such as "Which of God's miracles did you and your family celebrate?" and "What miracles of nature did you and your family discover?"

Tell kids that whenever you ring the *gold foil bell,* they are to stop talking, raise their hands, and focus on you. Explain that it's important to respond to this signal quickly so the class can do as many fun activities as possible.

ATTENTION GRABBER

STUCK IN THE MUD
(up to 10 minutes)

Have kids lie on the floor about 3 feet apart. Say: **Imagine that you've fallen into a mud pit. The mud is so thick and gooey, you can't move your legs. You can't bend your knees. You can't even wiggle your toes, but your ears are fine. Listen and follow these simple instructions without moving your legs.**

Give the following instructions one at a time. Allow time for kids to struggle with each instruction before you move on to the next one.

- ● **Sit up.**
- ● **Take off your shoes.**
- ● **Trade places with the person next to you.**
- ● **Stand up.**

After kids have tried to complete all the actions, ring the *gold foil bell.* Wait for kids to respond, then say: **You've just been miraculously freed from the mud pit. Please use your legs to get up and join me in a circle.**

After all the kids have joined the circle, ask:

● **What was it like to try to follow my instructions without moving your legs?** (Hard; frustrating; kind of fun.)

● **What was your reaction when I said you could move your legs again?** (I was relieved; I wanted to stretch.)

Say: **Most of you had a hard time moving around and getting up without using your legs. Imagine how you would feel if you had never been able to walk. When Jesus was on earth, he used his power to heal many people, including a man who couldn't walk.** 📖 **Jesus is able to take care of our hurts. We're going to talk more about Jesus' healing power today.**

TEACHER TIP

This lesson focuses on a story about a disabled man. Students with disabilities may react strongly to this lesson. They may wonder why Jesus hasn't healed them. Be sensitive to these responses and encourage disabled students to focus on other ways Jesus cares for them.

 the POINT

LEARNING LAB

the POINT

TEACHER TIP

Circulate among the groups and monitor the discussions. As soon as groups appear to be winding down, move on to the next series of questions so kids won't get bored or distracted.

> **I HATE IT WHEN THAT HAPPENS . . .**
> (up to 15 minutes)

Form groups of no more than four. Have each group choose a recorder who writes the group's responses on newsprint, a reporter to share the responses with the class, and one or more encouragers to encourage everyone to participate in the discussion. Distribute markers and newsprint, then say: ☞ **Jesus is able to take care of our hurts. Talk with the others in your group about some of your physical, or "outside" hurts. Maybe you've been kicked in the shins by a soccer teammate or you stubbed your toe on your front-porch step. If someone in your group shares something that's also happened to you, nod your head and say, "I hate it when that happens." Draw a line down the center of your newsprint and list your outside hurts on the left side of the page.**

Give kids a couple of minutes to discuss their physical hurts, then ring the *gold foil bell*. Wait for kids to respond, then say: **Now talk about your emotional or "inside" hurts. Maybe you had a fight with a friend, or your parents are getting a divorce. List your inside hurts on the right side of your newsprint.**

After several minutes, ring the *gold foil bell*. Wait for kids to respond, then ask reporters to share their groups' responses. After all the groups have had a chance to share, tape the sheets of newsprint to the wall. Have kids stand as you ask the following questions. Say: **Raise your hand when you've thought of an answer to each question. I'd like to hear lots of different, interesting answers. When someone gives an answer you've thought of and you don't have anything more to add, you may sit down. When everyone is seated, I'll ask you to stand again for the next question.**

Point to the outside hurts listed on the sheets of newsprint. Ask:

● **What's it like when one of these things happens to you?** (It hurts; I feel bad; I feel helpless.)

● **What do you do to help yourself feel better when one of these things happens?** (Get a Band-Aid; lie down and rest; take medicine.)

● **How can Jesus help you with your outside hurts?** (He can make me well again; he can help me to not be scared if I have to go to the doctor.)

Point to the inside hurts listed on the sheets of newsprint. Ask:

● **Which are worse: these inside hurts or the physical hurts we just talked about? Why?** (Inside hurts, because you keep them to yourself; physical hurts, because you just have to wait for them to get better.)

● **What do you do to help yourself feel better when one of these**

things happens? (Cry; punch my pillow; talk to someone; pray.)

● **How can Jesus help you with your inside hurts?** (He can help me to not feel angry; I don't feel so alone when I remember that Jesus is with me.)

Say: **God can turn our hurting to helping. Let me show you what I mean.** Distribute Bibles and have kids look up **2 Corinthians 1:3-5.** After everyone has found the passage, ask a volunteer to read it aloud. Ask:

● **According to these verses, what's the reason God allows us to hurt?** (So we'll be comforted; so we can comfort others when they're hurt.)

Say:  **Jesus is able to take care of our hurts, and he wants us to help others' hurts, too. We're going to hear about hurts that some kids your age actually experienced. After each person's story, we'll stop the tape and talk about ways we could help that person.**

Play the "That Really Hurts" segment of the *cassette tape.* Pause or stop the tape after each story and have kids discuss the following questions with a partner. Write the questions on a chalkboard or sheet of newsprint for easy reference.

● **What would you do if you experienced that kind of hurt?**
● **How could you help a friend who had that kind of hurt?**

Invite kids to share the responses they discussed with their partners. Then say: **Sometimes we feel so hurt that we can't think about anything else. But if we remember to reach out to Jesus, he'll help us.**  **Jesus is able to take care of our hurts. If we remember the comfort we get from Jesus, we'll be able to comfort our friends when they're hurt. Let's hear a story now about some men who brought their friend to Jesus to be healed.**

CARRIED AWAY
(up to 15 minutes)

On one side of the room, arrange chairs along three sides of a square to form a "house." Have kids form trios and line up on the other side of the room. Make sure the path to the house is clear.

Say: **Identify the youngest person in your trio. Starting right now, if you're the youngest person in your group, pretend you're paralyzed. You can't stand or move your legs. The others in your group will have to carry you to our house of chairs and set you gently on the floor. You may not move from the place where they set you. Listen to this story from Luke 5:17-26.** Open your Bible to the passage. **I'll tell you when it's time to carry the paralyzed people to the house.**

One day as Jesus was teaching the people, the Pharisees and teachers of the Law from every town in Galilee and Judea and from Jerusalem were there. Some men came carrying on a mat a man who was paralyzed. They tried to bring him in and put him down before Jesus. But because there were so many people there, they

 **the POINT**

 **the POINT**

KEY VERSE
CONNECTION

"Jesus answered, 'I am the way and the truth and the life. No one comes to the Father except through me' " **(John 14:6).**

Jesus wants people to be receptive of God's healing touch. Use the Key Verse to remind your kids that God's healing power comes from reaching out to Jesus and allowing him to help them with their emotional or physical pain.

couldn't find a way in. So they went up on the roof and lowered the man on his mat through the ceiling into the middle of the crowd right before Jesus.

Pause and show kids how to carry each other by creating a seat with their hands as shown in the margin illustration. Have kids transport their "paralytics" to the house of chairs. When all the kids are in the house, continue: **Seeing their faith, Jesus said, "Friend, your sins are forgiven." The Jewish teachers of the Law and the Pharisees grumbled and whispered among themselves.**

Whisper the following statement to two or three students and instruct them to pass it on: **Who does this man think he is? Only God can forgive sins!**

After the message has made its way through the "crowd," ask a student to repeat it aloud. Then say: **Even without hearing them talk, Jesus knew exactly what those Pharisees were thinking. Jesus said, "Why are you thinking these things? Which is easier: to say, 'Your sins are forgiven,' or to say, 'Stand up and walk'?"**

Say to the class: **Let's take a vote. Which of those things is easier to say?** Have kids vote by raising their hands. Count hands and announce the consensus before continuing.

Say: **Jesus didn't wait for the Pharisees to answer. He said, "I will prove to you that the Son of Man has authority on earth to forgive sins." So Jesus said to the paralyzed man, "I tell you, stand up, take your mat, and go home."**

One by one, help the "paralyzed" people up off the floor. Continue: **At once the man stood up before them, picked up his mat, and went home, praising God. All the people were fully amazed and began to praise God. They were filled with much respect and said, "Today we have seen amazing things!"** Close your Bible and say to the class: **Let's see everyone praise God by jumping and skipping all the way back to the other side of the room.**

When kids reach the other side of the room, ring the *gold foil bell*. Wait for kids to respond, then have them return to their trios to discuss the following questions. Write **"Luke 5:17-26"** on the blackboard and have Bibles available so kids can refer to the story. Say: **Discuss the following questions in your trios.** Pause after you ask each question to allow time for discussion. Ask:

● **Why do you think the Pharisees were grumbling and whispering to themselves?** (Because Jesus was more powerful than they were; because they didn't understand that Jesus was God.)

● **How do you think the paralyzed man felt when he heard the things the Pharisees were saying?** (Confused; mad; sad.)

● **Why do you think Jesus forgave the man's sins before he healed him?** (To prove he was God's Son; because the man was hurt by his sins, too.)

● **If you had been in the crowd that day, would you have believed Jesus could heal disease? Would you have believed he**

BIBLE *INSIGHT*

That Jesus recognized the faith of the paralytic's helpers (Luke 5:20) demonstrates the importance God places on the intercession of others. Yet Jesus directed God's forgiveness only to the paralytic, suggesting salvation was a strictly personal matter between him and Jesus.

LESSON SEVEN

could forgive sins? Why or why not? (I'd have believed Jesus could do anything because he made the man walk again; I wouldn't have been able to tell if Jesus had forgiven the man's sins.)

After kids have discussed the final question, ring the *gold foil bell*. Wait for kids to respond, then invite them to share the responses they discussed in their trios.

Say: **Sometimes our sins can hurt us as much as our physical injuries or diseases. Jesus knew the paralyzed man needed to be healed from the spiritual disease of sin in his life, as well as the physical condition. Jesus can help with the pain of sin in our lives, too.** **Jesus is able to take care of our hurts.**

 **the POINT**

LEARNING LAB

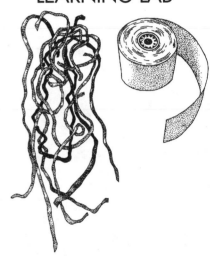

📖 FREE!
(up to 15 minutes)

Before class, write the text of **Romans 6:23** on a sheet of newsprint. Place the newsprint in a handy spot.

Say: **We may not be paralyzed in our bodies like the man in our story, but we can become paralyzed on the inside by sin in our lives. Just as the man's illness kept him from walking, our sin can keep us from having a good relationship with God.**

Give each student a *metallic ribbon,* a 6-inch piece of the *paper streamer roll,* and a pencil. Say: **On your piece of paper, write one wrong thing you've done this week. Maybe you talked back to your mom or sneaked a look at someone else's spelling test. Whatever you write on your paper will be between you and God. No one else will see it. When you're finished, fold your paper and place it in front of you.**

After all the kids have finished, say: **Now pick up your paper and hold it in your hands. I'm going to come around and tie your *metallic ribbon* around your wrists.**

As you tie each child's ribbon, say: **Sin separates us from God.** After you've tied all the ribbons, set a wastebasket in the front of the room. Post the newsprint with **Romans 6:23** written on it and lead the kids in reading the verse aloud.

Say: **Each of us deserves to be punished for the wrong things we've done. But Jesus took that punishment for us by dying on the cross. Because of Jesus' death and resurrection, our sins can be forgiven and we can look forward to living with God forever. Quietly get up and form a single-file line in front of the wastebasket. One at a time, step forward and throw your paper into the wastebasket after I cut your ribbon.**

As you cut each ribbon, say: **Jesus loves you and wants to forgive you.**

Gather kids in a circle and ask:

● **What was it like to have your wrists tied together?** (Frustrating; I felt like I was in jail.)

TEACHER TIP

If you have a large class, ask a volunteer to help you tie kids' wrists together.

● **What was it like when I cut the ribbons from your wrists?** (I was relieved; I felt free; it made me happy.)

● **How is that like the way you feel when God forgives you?** (I feel clean; I don't have to worry anymore about the wrong things I've done.)

the POINT

Say: **When we sin, we hurt ourselves, other people, and God. But** **Jesus is able to take care of our hurts. When Jesus forgives us, he forgets we ever committed that sin. And Jesus will always forgive us if we ask him to.**

Hands-On FUN AT HOME

We believe that Christian education extends beyond the classroom into the home. Photocopy the "Hands-On Fun at Home" handout (p. 91) for this week and send it home with your kids. Encourage kids to try several activities and discuss the Bible verses and questions with their parents.

CLOSING

BAND-AID PRAYERS
(up to 5 minutes)

Form pairs and give each student a Band-Aid. If you have an uneven number of students in your class, form one trio or pair up with the remaining student yourself. Say: **Look at the lists of outside and inside hurts we made earlier. Think about one of those hurts that's affecting you or someone you know and tell your partner about it.**

After two or three minutes, ring the *gold foil bell.* Wait for kids to respond, then say: **Now put your Band-Aid on your partner's arm. Wear your partner's Band-Aid this week. Each time you see it, remember to pray and ask Jesus to heal your partner's hurt. And remember that** **Jesus is able to take care of our hurts.**

the POINT

Close with a prayer similar to this one: **Dear God, thank you for sending Jesus to heal our hurts. Help us to share in that healing by praying for each other this week. In Jesus' name, amen.**

LESSON 7:
OUR HEALING GOD

the POINT ☞ **Jesus is able to take care of our hurts.**

BIBLE FOCUS

"Jesus answered, 'I am the way and the truth and the life. No one comes to the Father except through me' " (John 14:6).

WAY to PRAY

Gather your family together and talk about the hurts that each of you has experienced recently. Then make a commitment to pray for each other this week. Trace the door-hanger pattern from this paper onto construction paper or cardboard and cut it out. Decorate your door hanger any way you want and write, "We're praying for you today" on it. Each day, hang the door hanger on a different person's door. Remember to pray for that person!

FAITH walk

After dinner one night, work together to make a list of encouraging phrases. Include things like "Thanks for hanging in there," "That must have been awful," or "Is there anything I can do to help?" Hang the list on your refrigerator or in another visible place in your house. Use your encouraging phrases to comfort family members or friends when they're hurt.

CHECK it OUT

Read Mark 10:46-52.
Bartimaeus had faith Jesus could heal him, and he was healed. What hurts can you trust Jesus to heal?

Read Psalm 51:10-12.
Thank God for the joy of forgiveness.

CARE and SHARE

Because Jesus loves us and takes care of all our hurts, we can show love to others. This week, work with your family to make a care package for someone you know. You could make an "I miss you" package for a far-away family member, a "get well" box for an ailing neighbor, or an "I'm glad you're you" gift for your best friend.

Bake cookies or other goodies to put in your care package, and include a handmade card. Write a letter describing your favorite memory of the person you're sending the box to, and tuck in a few paper flowers or favorite candies.

LESSON 8

TAPPING INTO GOD'S POWER

"Jesus answered, 'I am the way and the truth and the life. No one comes to the Father except through me' "

(John 14:6).

THE POINT

☞ **Jesus' power comes from God.**

THE BIBLE BASIS

Luke 9:28-36. Jesus is transfigured.

Peter, James, and John accompanied Jesus to a mountaintop to pray. While they were there, the Transfiguration occurred. Jesus' face changed, and his clothing became shining white. Moses and Elijah appeared with Jesus, also in a glorious light. Scripture says they discussed Jesus' departure—or death—which would fulfill the law given by Moses and the prophesies of Elijah. A cloud enveloped Jesus, Moses, and Elijah, and a voice proclaimed, "This is my Son, whom I have chosen. Listen to him!" Matthew records that Peter, James, and John were terrified by this sequence of events and kept it to themselves.

One purpose of the Transfiguration was for Jesus' three closest disciples to see him in heavenly glory. Later they would understand that Jesus' life would fulfill both the Law and the prophesies.

Children can also find a wonderful message in this story. Kids often feel powerless in the face of adult authority. Life's events can be frightening and confusing. This lesson will help children understand that they're neither helpless nor alone. The same loving God who revealed Jesus' power can also provide power for their lives.

Other Scriptures used in this lesson are **Matthew 9:27-34; Mark 8:11-13; Luke 6:6-11; Acts 1:8; Galatians 5:22-23;** and **1 Peter 1:5-9.**

GETTING THE POINT

Students will
- understand that God can put his power in their lives,
- discuss ways to respond to people who doubt Jesus' power, and
- commit to relying on the Holy Spirit as their power source.

THIS LESSON AT A GLANCE

Before the lesson, collect the necessary items from the Learning Lab for the activities you plan to use. Refer to the pictures in the margin to see what each item looks like.

SECTION	MINUTES	WHAT STUDENTS WILL DO	LEARNING LAB SUPPLIES	CLASSROOM SUPPLIES
ATTENTION GRABBER	up to 10	**POWER SOURCE**—See light appear from an "unknown" source.	Light stick	
BIBLE EXPLORATION AND APPLICATION	up to 12	**GLORY!**—Read Luke 9:28-36 and act out the story.	Cassette: "Glory!"	Bibles, cassette player
	up to 20	**OH, YEAH?**—Read about observers of various miracles and discuss how to handle doubters.		Bibles, newsprint, marker
	up to 12	**POWER UP**—Read Galatians 5:22-23 and learn about the power of the Holy Spirit.		Bibles, paper, pencils
CLOSING	up to 6	**PEOPLE POWER**—Blow a pine cone around the room together and affirm that God can do powerful things.	Pine cone, light stick	

Hands-On FUN AT HOME

Remember to make photocopies of the "Hands-On Fun at Home" handout (p. 101) to send home with your kids. The "Fun at Home" handout suggests ways for kids to talk with their families about what they're learning in class and helps them put their faith into action.

THE LESSON

LEARNING LAB

As kids arrive, ask them which "Fun at Home" activities they tried. Ask questions such as "What is one hurt that you trusted Jesus to heal last week?" and "How did you or your family encourage someone else last week?"

Tell kids that whenever you ring the *gold foil bell,* they are to stop talking, raise their hands, and focus on you. Explain that it's important to respond to this signal quickly so the class can do as many fun activities as possible.

ATTENTION GRABBER

LEARNING LAB

POWER SOURCE
(up to 10 minutes)

Begin class by turning the lights off, on, then off again. Ask:
● **Where do these lights get their power?** (Electricity; by flipping the switch.)

Say: **I have something pretty surprising to show you. Follow me.** Lead kids to a darkened room. (Consider using a storage closet or windowless bathroom.) Then hold up the *light stick* and activate it by bending it in the center. Allow for oohs and ahs, then ask:
● **Where does this *light stick* get its power?** (I don't know; a chemical reaction.)

Pass the *light stick* around. As kids are examining it, say: **We can't see the power source behind this *light stick*, but we can see the light it creates. We can't see or understand God's power, but we can see the results of God's power in the amazing miracles Jesus performed.** ☞ **Jesus' power comes from God. We're going to learn more about God's power in our lesson today.**

 the POINT

Lead kids back to the classroom. Place the *light stick* out of sight for use in the closing activity. It will keep glowing for a few hours, so you may need to put it in a closet or another enclosed area to keep kids from being distracted.

BIBLE EXPLORATION AND APPLICATION

LEARNING LAB

GLORY!
(up to 12 minutes)

Form pairs. Say: **We're going to look at an amazing display of God's power from the Bible.** Distribute Bibles and help kids find **Luke 9:28-36.** Have kids read the story together. Encourage them to take turns reading.

After kids have finished reading the story, ring the *gold foil bell* and wait for kids to respond. Say: **Now we're going to travel back to the time this story took place. As we listen to the story on the *cassette tape*, let's bring the story to life with our actions. Each time you hear the name Peter, James, or John, I want you to yawn. Let's practice that.**

Repeat the three names and let students practice yawning. Then continue: **Since Moses and Elijah came down from heaven in this story, whenever you hear the name Moses or Elijah, fan your hands around your face. Let's practice that.**

Repeat the two names and let students practice fanning their hands around their faces. Then say: **I'll need a volunteer to play Jesus.** Select a volunteer, then continue: **Each time the name Jesus is spoken on the *cassette tape*, raise your arms toward heaven.**

Play the "Glory!" segment of the *cassette tape* as kids do the actions you've assigned.

After the story, have kids give themselves a big round of applause for their participation. Then have everyone stand. Say: **Raise your hand when you've thought of an answer to each question I ask. I'd like to hear lots of different, interesting answers. When someone gives a response you've thought of and you don't have anything more to add, you may sit down. When everyone is seated, I'll ask you to stand again for the next question.** Ask:

● **What thoughts might have been in the disciples' minds when they saw Jesus' clothes become shining white?** (That this was another miracle; that Jesus really was God's Son.)

Say: **When Peter saw that Jesus was standing with Moses and Elijah, he offered to make a tent for each of them.** Ask:

● **What would you do in that situation?** (Stand back and watch; ask Moses a question about the Ten Commandments.)

● **Why do you think the disciples were afraid when the cloud covered them?** (Because it was dark; because the voice was loud; because they thought they might be in trouble.)

● **Why do you think God spoke from the cloud?** (To make sure the disciples knew Jesus was God's Son; to remind the disciples to listen to Jesus.)

Say: **Peter, James and John saw special power in Jesus when his appearance changed. When they heard God's voice from the cloud, they knew that Jesus' power comes from God.**

the POINT

BIBLE INSIGHT

Scholars debate the significance of the appearance of Moses and Elijah during the Transfiguration. Some suggest they were simply representative of Old Testament laws and prophecy. Others suggest Moses, as predecessor of the Messiah, represented the past while Elijah, who predicted the end times, represented the future.

OH, YEAH?
(up to 20 minutes)

Before class, write the following questions on a sheet of newsprint. (Possible answers are provided here for your reference.)

● What did Jesus do? (Healed people; drove out a demon.)

● How did people respond? (They said Jesus got his power from the devil; they got mad.)

● Why do you think people reacted that way? (They were jealous of Jesus; they were trying to convince other people not to believe in Jesus.)

Say: **After being with Jesus on the mountain, it was easy for Peter, James and John to believe that**  **Jesus' power comes from God. Let's find out how some other people responded to Jesus' power.**

Have kids form two groups by numbering off by twos. Post the sheet of newsprint, then say: **Let's look at some ways Jesus used his power and at how people responded to Jesus. If you're a #1, go to the right side of the room and look up Matthew 9:27-34. Then find a partner on your side of the room and discuss the questions on the newsprint. If you're a #2, go to the left side of the room and look up Luke 6:6-11. Then find a partner on your side of the room and discuss the questions on the newsprint.**

After kids have had time to look up the Scriptures and discuss the questions, call for their attention by ringing the *gold foil bell*. Wait for kids to respond, then say: **Now find a new partner from the opposite side of the room. Tell that new partner what happened in your passage and compare the ways people responded. Were they the same or different? Why?**

After two or three minutes, ring the *gold foil bell* to bring everyone together. Invite kids to share the similarities and differences they discussed with their partners. Say: **Now let's see how the Pharisees responded to Jesus.** Have kids look up **Mark 8:11-13.** Ask a volunteer to read the passage aloud, then ask:

● **Why do you think the Pharisees approached Jesus?** (Because they'd heard about his miracles; because they were curious.)

● **What was Jesus' response to the Pharisees' request?** (He sighed; he went away.)

● **Why do you think Jesus refused to do a miracle for the Pharisees?** (Because Jesus knew they wouldn't believe in him anyway; because Jesus wanted them to trust him.)

Say: **Before Jesus came, the people listened to the Pharisees' teachings. But when people heard about Jesus, they began to follow him and listen to him instead. This made the Pharisees very jealous, and they were always looking for ways to trick Jesus or make him look bad. They wanted to make people doubt that**  **Jesus' power comes from God. But Jesus knew what they were up to, and he never let their doubting or tricks keep him from using his power to help and heal people.**

Sometimes we may encounter people today who doubt Jesus' power. We shouldn't let other people's doubts keep us from believing in Jesus' power. I'll show you why.

Have kids look up **1 Peter 1:5-9.** Have a volunteer read the passage aloud as other kids follow along in their Bibles. Then ask:

TEACHER TIP

It's important to say The Point just as it's written during each activity. Repeating The Point over and over will help kids remember it and apply it to their lives.

the POINT

● **What is it like knowing that the same power that helped Jesus do miracles is protecting you through your faith?** (Great; surprising; exciting.)

● **Tell about a time you felt really happy because of your faith.** (When I prayed for my mom to get better, and she did; when my best friend started coming to church with me.)

● **How can the joy you get from your faith help you believe in Jesus even when other people doubt?** (I know I'll be happier if I keep believing in Jesus; it makes me want to help other people believe in Jesus so they'll be happy, too.)

Say: **Jesus' power comes from God. It's exciting to know that if we believe in Jesus, that same power is available to us today. Let's learn more about tapping into God's power for our lives.**

POWER UP
(up to 12 minutes)

Help kids form groups of four. Distribute pencils and paper. Have each group choose a timekeeper, a recorder to write down the group's ideas, a reporter to share the ideas with the class, and an encourager to make sure everyone in the group participates. Say: **In your group of four, talk about times when it's hard to follow God. Maybe you have a hard time praying, or you're afraid to tell your friends about Jesus. Take one minute to list those times on your paper.**

After one minute, ring the *gold foil bell.* Wait for kids to respond, then invite groups to share their responses. Ask:

● **Why is it sometimes hard to follow God?** (Because other people might make fun of me; because there are a lot of things to remember to do.)

the POINT

● **Would it be easier for you to follow God if you knew you didn't have to do it alone? Why or why not?** (Yes, because I could ask my friends to help me when it's hard; no, it would still be hard.)

Say: **Jesus' power comes from God. When Jesus was on earth, he performed many miracles through God's power. When Jesus went up to be with God in heaven, his disciples wondered if God's power would be available to them. In Acts 1:8, Jesus promised his disciples that they would receive power through the Holy Spirit. The Holy Spirit is God's special gift to Christians. The Holy Spirit comforts us, guides us, and helps us grow in our faith. And the Holy Spirit gives us power we need to follow God even when it's hard.**

Have kids remain in their groups of four. Say: **Think back to our discussion of the fruits of the Spirit.** Distribute Bibles and have kids look up **Galatians 5:22-23.** Assign each group one or more fruits of the Spirit and have students discuss how their fruit(s) could help them when it's hard to follow God.

After several minutes, ring the *gold foil bell.* Wait for kids to respond, then ask:

TEACHER TIP

This lesson touches on the Holy Spirit only briefly. If kids are curious to know more, refer them to John 14:16-21 or John 16:13. Kids will learn more about the Holy Spirit in future Hands-On Bible Curriculum lessons.

● **How can the fruits of the Holy Spirit help you follow God?** (The Holy Spirit can help me be patient with my little brother; the Holy Spirit can help me be peaceful instead of fighting on the playground.)

Say: **Trusting the Holy Spirit is one of the best ways to tap into God's power. To help us remember to trust the Holy Spirit this week, let's make up hand signs to represent the fruits of the Spirit. Work with the people in your group to come up with a hand sign for your group's fruit(s). For example, if your group talked about love, your sign might be putting your hand over your heart or hugging yourself. If your group talked about gentleness, your sign might be rocking your arms as if you were rocking a baby.**

Give kids several minutes to come up with their signs, then have them stand and present their signs as you read the verses from Galatians once more.

Say: ☞ **Jesus' power comes from God. We can have that same power in our lives by trusting the Holy Spirit to help us. Use the signs you made up to help you remember all the ways the Holy Spirit helps us.**

the POINT

Hands-On FUN AT HOME

We believe that Christian education extends beyond the classroom into the home. Photocopy the "Hands-On Fun at Home" handout (p. 101) for this week and send it home with your kids. Encourage kids to try several activities and discuss the Bible verses and questions with their parents.

CLOSING

PEOPLE POWER
(up to 5 minutes)

Have kids kneel in a circle. Place a *pine cone* from the Learning Lab in front of one student. Say: **I'd like you to blow this *pine cone* around the circle.**

Let the student blow on the *pine cone* several times, then say: **I think (name) looks out of breath. Let's all help blow the *pine cone* around.**

Pick up the *pine cone* and begin blowing it around the circle to your left, letting each student have a turn.

When the *pine cone* comes back to you, pick it up and say: ☞ **Jesus' power comes from God. God can do powerful things through one person, but God's power is multiplied when Christians work together. So if you're feeling low on power this week, link up with another Christian friend and tap into God's power together.**

LEARNING LAB

the POINT

TAPPING INTO GOD'S POWER

Have kids stand in a circle and pass the *light stick* from person to person as each student says, "God's power is at work in you." Have kids continue around the circle until the *light stick* comes back to you. Close by praying. **Thank you God, for giving us your power. Amen.**

Collect the *pine cone* and the *light stick*.

LESSON 8:
TAPPING INTO GOD'S POWER

the POINT ☞ **Jesus' power comes from God.**

▪ ▪ ▪ ▪ ▪ ▪ ▪ ▪ ▪ ▪ ▪ ▪

BIBLE FOCUS

"Jesus answered, 'I am the way and the truth and the life. No one comes to the Father except through me' " (John 14:6).

Hands-On FUN!
AT HOME

CHECK it OUT

Read Romans 8:11.
What does God give us power to do?

Read James 5:13-16.
What great things have happened because of your prayers?

FAITH walk

Take a family "power walk" to explore the power sources at your house. Walk through each room and count how many electrical outlets, light switches, or lamps you find. Don't forget to visit the furnace, water heater, and fuse box. After your power walk, try living for an evening without using any power sources such as gasoline, natural gas, or electricity. How is that like living without God's power?

WAY to PRAY

Wrap an extension cord around a Bible. Pass the Bible around and have each member of your family tell about a time that God has shown his power in your family. After each person has had a turn, have everyone put one hand on the Bible and "tap into" the power of prayer. Thank God for all the powerful things he's done for your family.

MINUTE mysteries

Stand in a doorway and put your wrists on the doorjambs. Press your wrists against the doorjambs as you count to 30 very slowly. When you step out of the doorway and drop your arms, they'll rise all by themselves. How is that like God's power?

LESSON

9

DOWN WITH DEATH!

▪ ▪ ▪ ▪ ▪ ▪ ▪ ▪ ▪ ▪ ▪ ▪ ▪ ▪

for Lessons 6–9 **KEY** *VERSE*

"Jesus answered, 'I am the way and the truth and the life. No one comes to the Father except through me' "

(John 14:6).

THE POINT

☞ **Jesus has power over death.**

THE BIBLE BASIS

John 11:1-44. Jesus raises Lazarus.

Shortly before his death on the cross, Jesus was summoned to Bethany to visit a sick friend. Mary and Martha knew their brother had taken a turn for the worse, but they trusted that Jesus could heal him. Instead of leaving for Bethany right away, Jesus waited two days. By the time Jesus arrived, Lazarus had died. Jesus was greeted with cries of "You should have been here sooner!" But cries of doubt quickly changed to joy and wonder when Jesus called Lazarus back from the tomb. In his last re-corded earthly miracle, Jesus proved that he did indeed have the power to give life—for now and for eternity.

Third- and fourth-graders need to know the comfort of Jesus' life-giv-ing power. By this age, many kids have experienced the death of a family member, friend, or pet. With this experience come many questions: What happens to people after they die? Do they go to heaven? Is it OK to be sad about death? For how long? This lesson will help your students dis-cover that death isn't the end after all. Students will be comforted to learn that, for those who believe in Jesus, death leads to glorious resurrection.

Other Scriptures used in this lesson are **Mark 5:21-42; Luke 7:11-17; John 14:1-3; Romans 8:38-39;** and **Revelation 21:3-4, 21-24.**

GETTING THE POINT

Students will
- share their feelings about death and dying,
- learn about people Jesus raised from death, and
- discover the hope they have in heaven.

THIS LESSON AT A GLANCE

Before the lesson, collect the necessary items from the Learning Lab for the activities you plan to use. Refer to the pictures in the margin to see what each item looks like.

SECTION	MINUTES	WHAT STUDENTS WILL DO	LEARNING LAB SUPPLIES	CLASSROOM SUPPLIES
ATTENTION GRABBER	up to 12	**MISSING YOU**—Write or draw things they remember about people who have died.		Paper, markers
BIBLE EXPLORATION AND APPLICATION	up to 12	**COME FORTH!**—Act out the story of Lazarus from John 11:1-44.	Paper streamer roll	Bibles
	up to 12	**PANICKING PARENTS**—Read about two children Jesus raised from death.		Bibles
	up to 12	**HOPE OF HEAVEN**—Hear a story about heaven and discuss John 14:1-3; Romans 8:38-39; and Revelation 21:3-4, 21-24.	Cassette: "The Unlit Candle"	Bibles, chalkboard and chalk or newsprint and marker, cassette player, paper, markers
CLOSING	up to 12	**REMEMBER ME**—Write positive things they'll remember about classmates.		Copies of "Terrific Tombstones" handout (p. 111), markers, tape

Remember to make photocopies of the "Hands-On Fun at Home" handout (p. 112) to send home with your kids. The "Fun at Home" handout suggests ways for kids to talk with their families about what they're learning in class and helps them put their faith into action.

THE LESSON

As kids arrive, ask them which "Fun at Home" activities they tried. Ask questions such as "What was it like to do without power in your house for a little while? What would it be like to do without God's power in our lives?" and "What are some ways God has shown his power in your family recently?"

Explain to kids that whenever you ring the *gold foil bell,* they are to stop talking, raise their hands, and focus on you. Explain that it's important to respond to this signal quickly so the class can do as many fun activities as possible.

MODULE REVIEW

Use the casual interaction time at the beginning of class to ask kids the following module-review questions.

● **How has Jesus helped heal your hurts?**

● **How did the power of the Holy Spirit help you last week?**

● **What's your favorite miracle we've learned about in the past few weeks? Why?**

● **How is your life different as a result of what we've learned in class this month?**

ATTENTION GRABBER

MISSING YOU
(up to 12 minutes)

Before class, set out paper and markers. When most of your class has arrived, say: **Think of someone you know who has died. It could be a grandparent or another relative, a friend, or even a pet. If you don't know someone, think about someone you've read about in the newspaper or in a book. Write or draw a picture of something you remember about that person.**

As kids are working, circulate to make sure they aren't interfering with one another's work. This should be a fairly quiet activity. After about five minutes, ring the *gold foil bell.* Wait for kids to respond, then ask for volunteers to share their memories. If kids are slow to volunteer, share a memory of your own to get them started. Then draw kids out by asking questions such as "Has anyone else had a grandmother die?" or "What was your favorite thing about your relative?"

After several volunteers have shared, ask:

● **How did you feel when the person you wrote about or drew a picture of died?** (Sad; angry; upset; afraid.)

● **Did you experience those same feelings as you thought about that person today? Explain.** (Yes, thinking about her just made me sad

TEACHER TIP

If you have space in your classroom, have kids spread out for this activity. Kids may feel self-conscious about sharing their memories if other kids are looking over their shoulders.

TEACHER TIP

Death is a sensitive and even scary subject for many third- and fourth-graders. As you teach this lesson, be sensitive to kids' feelings. Don't force them to share their feelings if it makes them uncomfortable. Be especially sensitive to children who have come in contact with death recently.

DOWN WITH DEATH!

all over again; no, thinking about him made me happy because I remembered all the fun times we had.)

Say: **When someone we know dies, we have lots of strong feelings. Sometimes we're sad and miss that person. If someone dies after being sick for a long time, we may be happy that person doesn't have any more pain. We may even feel angry at the person for dying and leaving us. But, as Christians, we know we haven't lost that person forever if he or she believed in Jesus because Jesus has power over death. We're going to learn more about what that means today.**

the POINT

LEARNING LAB

BIBLE EXPLORATION AND APPLICATION

COME FORTH!
(up to 12 minutes)

Say: **Jesus had a good friend who died, too. Back in Jesus' time, they wrapped people who had died in pieces of cloth before they buried them. We'll pretend to wrap someone using our *paper streamer roll*. Who'd like to volunteer to be wrapped up today?** Choose a child to be wrapped up, then continue: **We're going to pretend that** (name of volunteer) **is Jesus' friend Lazarus. As we take turns reading parts of this story, we'll wrap the *paper streamer roll* around our volunteer. We'll need to be careful not to wrap our volunteer too tightly.**

Distribute Bibles and help kids look up **John 11:1-40.** Assign each student two to four verses. After each child reads, help him or her loosely wrap the *paper streamer roll* around "Lazarus" once. Make sure all the kids get a turn to read verses and to wrap Lazarus.

When you've completed the last wrap after verse 40, tear the paper from the roll and darken your classroom as much as possible. Ring the *gold foil bell* and wait for kids to respond. Help your wrapped-up Lazarus lie down in the center of the room. Say: **Lazarus was buried in a cave-like tomb. Let's imagine how dark and quiet it must have been by lying down, closing our eyes, and not talking at all for 30 seconds.**

After about 30 seconds, have kids sit up. Whisper to Lazarus that when you say, "Lazarus, come out!" you want him or her to rip through the *paper streamer roll*, stand up, and walk. Have the rest of the kids stand in a circle around Lazarus. Say: **The next part of the story gets pretty exciting, so listen carefully.**

Read verses 41-43 aloud to the kids. Pause after you say, "Lazarus, come out!" to allow your volunteer to break through the *paper streamer roll*. Read verse 44, then pick up the ripped paper wrapping. Say: **I'll ask some questions. Raise your hand when you've thought of an answer to each question I ask. I'd like to hear lots of different,**

TEACHER TIP

If your volunteer has trouble breaking free from the wrapping, help him or her get started by tearing through a few strips.

interesting answers. When someone gives an answer you've thought of and you don't have anything more to add, you may sit down. When everyone is seated, I'll ask you to stand again for the next question. Ask:

● **What do you think Mary and Martha thought when Jesus didn't come right away?** (That he didn't care; that he was too busy.)

● **Why do you think Jesus cried when he saw Lazarus' tomb?** (Because Lazarus was his friend; because the tomb reminded him that Lazarus was really dead.)

● **How do you think Mary and Martha felt about opening Lazarus' tomb?** (Scared; worried about the smell; curious about why Jesus wanted them to open it.)

● **How do you think Lazarus felt when he opened his eyes and discovered he was all wrapped up in a dark cave?** (Scared; confused; he probably wondered how he got there.)

● **What do you think the people watching thought when they saw Lazarus coming out of the tomb?** (They thought he was a ghost; they thought they were seeing things; they were amazed.)

Say: **The people who gathered around Lazarus' tomb were sure that Lazarus was dead. But Jesus said, "I am the resurrection and the life," and he was able to bring Lazarus back to life. That's because**  **Jesus has power over death.**

PANICKING PARENTS
(up to 12 minutes)

Say: **Lazarus wasn't the only person Jesus raised from the dead. Jesus also raised two children from the dead. Let's find out more.**

Have kids form two groups by numbering off by twos. Say: **If you're a #1, go to the right side of the room and look up Mark 5:21-42. Then find a partner on your side of the room and take turns reading the verses in the passage. If you're a #2, go to the left side of the room and look up Luke 7:11-17. Then find a partner on your side of the room and take turns reading the verses in the passage.**

After kids have had time to read their passages, call for their attention by ringing the *gold foil bell*. Wait for kids to respond, then say: **Now find a new partner from the opposite side of the room. Tell that new partner what happened in your passage and discuss the following questions.**

Pause after you ask each question to give kids time for discussion. Ask:

● **What would you have thought if you'd seen Jesus raise a boy or girl from the dead?** (I would have wondered if the girl were really dead or just sleeping; I would have been amazed; I would have believed in Jesus right away.)

● **If you were a friend of the girl or boy Jesus raised, what's the first thing you'd say to your friend?** (I'd ask her what it felt like to be dead; I'd tell him I was glad he was alive again.)

It's important to say The Point just as it's written during each activity. Repeating The Point over and over will help kids remember it and apply it to their lives.

✍ the POINT

KEY VERSE
CONNECTION

"Jesus answered, 'I am the way and the truth and the life. No one comes to the Father except through me' " (John 14:6).

Kids might not relate to the Lazarus story if they've had a loved one die who has not been raised from the dead. Use the Key Verse to help them understand how a relationship with Jesus gives us eternal life.

● **How do you think the parents felt when Jesus raised their children from the dead?** (Excited; surprised; grateful.)

● **What do you think the parents told other people about Jesus afterward?** (That he was great; that he was powerful; that he could do miracles.)

After two or three minutes, ring the *gold foil bell*. Invite kids to share the responses they discussed with their partners.

Say: **The parents in these stories believed that Jesus could raise their children, and he did. We know that** **Jesus has power over death. If our friends and family believe in Jesus, we'll see them again in heaven. Let's talk more about heaven now.**

the POINT

LEARNING LAB

HOPE OF HEAVEN
(up to 12 minutes)

Write the following Scripture references on a chalkboard or newsprint: **John 14:1-3; Romans 8:38-39; Revelation 21:3-4; Revelation 21:21-24.** Say: **We're going to listen to a tape about one man's idea of heaven. Then we'll see what the Bible has to say.**

Play "The Unlit Candle" from the *cassette tape*. This story about death and heaven is adapted from Jewish folklore. It's a touching story of a father who dreams of his only daughter in heaven with an unlit candle because his tears and sadness about her death put the candle out.

Stop or pause the cassette player after the break in the story. Ask:

● **What would you do for this father who was sad because his daughter had died?** (Tell him about heaven; pray for him; try to cheer him up.)

Continue with the *cassette tape*.

Say: **This story tells us how one person imagined heaven. With a partner, look up one of the passages I've written on the newsprint. Then have pairs answer the following questions and take turns reporting their thoughts to the class.** Ask:

● **What does the Bible tell us that heaven will be like?** (Jesus will be there with us; we'll never be separated from God's love there; the streets will be made of gold.)

● **In our story, Hannah was sad; do you think people are really sad in heaven? Explain.** (No, because everyone's happy in heaven; yes, because they know people miss them.)

Say: **The Bible tells us that there is no sadness in heaven. So Hannah would never be sad there. Like Hannah's father, we may miss people who have died, but if those people loved Jesus, we know they're happy in heaven.** Ask:

● **Who are you most looking forward to seeing in heaven?** (My grandmother; Jesus; my aunt.)

● **Does knowing you'll see someone again in heaven make it easier to say goodbye when that person dies? Explain.** (Yes, because

I'm happy that they get to go to heaven; no, even though I know they'll be in heaven I'll still miss them.)

Say: **It's OK to be sad when someone dies, especially if that person was a family member or close friend. Jesus was sad when Lazarus died. But as Christians, we don't have to keep crying and being sad forever. Because Jesus died and rose again, we know if we believe in Jesus we'll rise again, too. We can look forward to heaven because we believe in Jesus.** Jesus has power over death, and he's promised to prepare a place for us to live with him in heaven forever.

the POINT

Hands-On We believe that Christian education extends beyond the classroom into the home. Photocopy the "Hands-On Fun at Home" handout (p. 112) for this week and send it home with your kids. Encourage kids to try several activities and discuss the Bible verses and questions with their parents.

CLOSING

REMEMBER ME
(up to 12 minutes)

Tape copies of the "Terrific Tombstones" handout (p. 111) to a wall of your classroom. Make sure you tape up a copy for each student.

Say: **Sometimes we have time to prepare for people dying, but other times people die suddenly. When someone dies suddenly, people often wish they had had a chance to tell that person how special he or she was. We're going to take an opportunity to do that right now, while we're all alive and kicking!**

Distribute markers. Say: **When people are buried, their graves are usually marked with tombstones. Often tombstones list special things about the people buried there, such as "beloved child" or "loving husband and father." Go to the handouts on the wall and decorate your own tombstone. Make sure your name is on your paper somewhere.**

Give kids several minutes to complete their tombstones, then ring the *gold foil bell.* Wait for kids to respond. Say: **Take a few minutes to write things you appreciate about the people in our class on their tombstones. You might write things like "I appreciate your smile," or "I appreciate your good sense of humor."**

Give kids several minutes to write words of appreciation on one another's tombstones, then ring the *gold foil bell.* Wait for kids to respond, then have them remove their tombstones from the wall and form a circle.

TEACHER TIP

Encourage kids to write on as many tombstones as possible. If some tombstones seem to have few affirmations, write on them yourself.

DOWN WITH DEATH!

Say: **Trade tombstones with the person next to you. We'll go around the circle, and each of us will read something special about someone else. When it's your turn, say the person's name, then say, "I'll always remember your special smile," or whatever you think is special about that person.**

After everyone has been affirmed, close by praying: **Dear God, we thank you that  Jesus has power over death. We look forward to the hope of heaven, where we'll see our friends who love you and we'll celebrate new life together. In Jesus' name, amen.**

the POINT

TERRIFIC TOMBSTONES

"I am the resurrection and the life. He who believes in me will live, even though he dies" (John 11:25).

Hands-On FUN AT HOME

LESSON 9:
DOWN WITH DEATH!

the POINT ☞ Jesus has power over death.

BIBLE FOCUS

"Jesus answered, 'I am the way and the truth and the life. No one comes to the Father except through me'" (John 14:6).

PACKED with POWER

Before dinner one night, try this experiment with your family. Place a potato on the kitchen counter. Hold a plastic drinking straw near the top, leaving the top opening uncovered. Raise the straw about five inches above the potato, then quickly try to stick the end of the straw into the potato. The straw will crumple.

Now try the experiment again with a different straw, but this time hold your thumb over the top of the straw. The second straw will easily pierce the potato, proving more powerful than the first.

Just as the first straw lacked power, without Jesus we lack power over death. But just as the second straw was packed with power, Jesus has power over death.

FAITH walk

Declare a "Heavenly Friends" night. After dinner, gather your family together and talk about people you'll look forward to seeing in heaven. You could talk about friends, relatives, famous people, or Bible characters you'd like to meet. Share fun things you remember about them and things you'd like to ask or tell them when you see them in heaven.

FUN food

Ask a parent to help you make an angel food cake from a mix. Cut the cake into bite-sized pieces and put it in a bowl. Pass the bowl around the table and have family members tell about one thing they're looking forward to in heaven as they take a piece of cake.

CHECK it OUT

Read Job 19:25-27.
What's the first thing you want to ask God when you see him in heaven?

Read 2 Corinthians 5:1.
What do you think your heavenly body will be like?

Read Revelation 21:19-21.
What do you think heaven will look like?

JESUS, OUR FRIEND
■ ■ ■ ■ ■ ■ ■ ■ ■ ■ ■ ■

Friendships are an important part of life, no matter our age. For 8- and 9-year-olds, developing lasting friendships is a new and exciting adventure. These kids are no longer willing to pal around the playground with the nearest interested partner. Instead, many third- and fourth-graders have established relationships with one or more steady friends. Most kids are extremely loyal to their friends and will do everything they can to make sure their friends are happy. Friends' approval may even become more important than the approval of parents or other adults.

Third- and fourth-graders are anxious to make friends, but they'll need guidance to develop healthy friendships that will last. These four lessons will teach kids the qualities that contribute to solid friendships. By looking at Jesus' example, kids will learn how to comfort each other when they're sad or afraid. They'll learn how to build loyalty in friendships and how real friends handle disappointment. Use these lessons to show kids that Jesus is a real friend, and if they follow his example, they can be real friends, too.

JESUS, OUR FRIEND

LESSON	PAGE	THE POINT	THE BIBLE BASIS
10—STICKING TOGETHER	119	Real friends stick up for each other.	Luke 19:1-10
11—REACHING OUT	127	Real friends comfort each other when they're sad.	Mark 6:45-51
12—POSITIVE PEERS	137	Real friends don't ask you to do things that are wrong.	John 15:12-17
13—ALL-WEATHER FRIENDS	147	Real friends still love you, even if you disappoint them.	Luke 22:54-62; John 21:15-17

LEARNING LAB

LEARNING LAB

TEACHER TIP

Prepare extra "generic" message cards or supplement the *care cards* with index cards.

LEARNING LAB

THE SIGNAL

During the lessons on Jesus, our friend, the signal to bring kids back together during activities will be to ring the *gold foil bell* found in the Learning Lab. In response to ringing the bell, have kids stop what they're doing, raise their hands, and focus on you.

Tell kids about this signal—and practice it—before the lesson begins. Explain that it's important to respond to this signal quickly so the class can do as many fun activities as possible. During the lessons, you'll be prompted when to use the signal.

THE TIME STUFFER

This module's Time Stuffer will encourage kids to strengthen their friendships with one another. To set up the Secret Pals Center, write each student's name on a slip of paper. Put the slips of paper in a bag or box. Set the bag or box, the *care cards,* and markers on a table near the "Secret Pals" poster. You'll find the *care cards* and poster in the Learning Lab. During their free moments, kids may choose a secret pal by pulling a name out of the bag or box. Kids may either choose a new secret pal each week or keep the same secret pal for the whole module. Using ideas from the "Secret Pals" poster, kids may write encouraging messages to their secret pals on the *care cards*. At the end of each class, pass out the cards and watch kids' friendships grow. When you've finished all four lessons, be sure to have secret pals identify themselves.

REMEMBERING THE BIBLE

Each four- or five-week module focuses on a key Bible verse. The key verse for this module is **"My command is this: Love each other as I have loved you" (John 15:12).**

Following are two activities you may do with your third- and fourth-graders to help them remember this Bible verse and apply it to their lives.

TESTAMENT OF LOVE

Use this activity at the beginning of the module to start kids thinking about love and friendship or use it at the end to help them sum up what they've learned. Before class, write the following questions on a sheet of newsprint and hang it in your classroom. Possible answers are provided for your reference.

● **Who are some people you love?** (Parents; friends; brothers and sisters.)

● **Who are some people who love you?** (Parents; Jesus; grandparents; friends.)

● **What do those people do to show they love you?** (My parents take care of me; my friends do nice things for me; Jesus died for me.)

Form pairs, then distribute sheets of newsprint and markers or crayons. Say: **With your partner, draw a picture or write about a scene that describes what love means to you. For example, you might draw or write about family members helping each other. To help you think of ideas, discuss the questions on the newsprint with your partner.**

After several minutes ring the *gold foil bell*. Wait for kids to respond, then invite pairs to share their pictures or stories with the class. After all the pairs have shared, tape the pictures or stories to the wall to create a mural. Ask:

● **Why is it important for us to love one another?** (So nobody gets hurt; to make each other feel good.)

Open your Bible to **John 15:12** and say: **In John 15:12, Jesus commands us to love one another. But he doesn't just *tell* us to love one another—his example *shows* us how to love. The New Testament tells us many stories about times Jesus showed love to others. The pictures and stories you've just created tell us about ways we can show love today. Let's write Jesus' words about love on our mural.**

Read the verse again and have each student write one word from the verse along the top of the mural. If you have more than 12 students in your class, write the verse twice, once along the top and once along the bottom of the mural. When kids have finished writing the verse, lead them in repeating it together. Close the activity by singing "This Is My Commandment" with the *cassette tape*. Use the "Lyrics Poster" in the Learning Lab to assist you.

VALENTINE BINGO

LEARNING LAB

Form two teams and give each person a copy of the "Valentine Bingo" handout (p. 117). Say: **Valentine's Day is a great opportunity to let our friends know we care about them. But we don't have to wait for Valentine's Day to show love for one another. Each square on your handout tells one way you can show love for other people. You'll have five minutes to complete as many squares as you can. The team that completes the most squares will get a prize. Ready? Go!**

After five minutes, ring the *gold foil bell*. Wait for kids to respond, then have teams count their completed squares. Identify the winning team, then lead the other team in giving a group hug as a prize. Have kids sit in a circle, then ask:

● **How did the actions on your cards help you show love?** (I

Boys and girls may be a little squeamish about hugging each other. Tell kids this is a happy hug, not a mushy hug. (You may also need to remind them not to squeeze the winning team too hard.)

talked to people I didn't know very well; I said nice things to people.)

● **What are other ways you can show love for your family and friends?** (Help my mom with the dishes; help my brother clean up his room; play with someone who's new at school.)

● **How can you show love for Jesus?** (By doing what he wants me to do; by going to church; by praying.)

Say: **Jesus said, "This is my command: Love each other as I have loved you." Let's repeat that verse together**. Pause for kids to repeat the verse, then continue: **The actions we did in our Bingo game and the things we just talked about are only a few of the ways we can show love to our family, friends, and others. Let's remember to obey Jesus' command and show love to other people this week.**

Close by singing "This Is My Commandment." Use the *cassette tape* and the "Lyrics Poster" from the Learning Lab to assist you.

Valentine Bingo

Complete as many of the following instructions as you can in the time allowed. After you complete each instruction, get the initials of the person who helped you complete it.

Give a pat on the back to someone younger than you.
_____

Shake hands with someone from another school.
_____

Give a high five to someone of the opposite sex.
_____

Give a big smile to your teacher.
_____

Tell someone who's wearing blue one thing you like about your best friend.
_____

Give a hug to someone you know really well.
_____

Tell someone you don't know very well that you're glad he or she came.
_____

Tell someone older than you that Jesus loves him or her.
_____

Tell someone who's wearing white why you think he or she would make a good friend.
_____

Give a compliment to someone who's wearing shoes with shoelaces.
_____

Scratch the back of someone who's wearing a watch or other jewelry.
_____

Tell someone with dark hair one of your favorite things to do with a friend.
_____

Tell someone with long hair how you'll show love for your mom this week.
_____

Tell someone with short hair how you'll show love for your dad this week.
_____

Tell someone who's wearing red why you like your favorite relatives.
_____

Tell someone who's wearing green why you like your brother or sister.
_____

"My command is this: Love each other as I have loved you" (John 15:12).

LESSON 10
STICKING TOGETHER

for Lessons 10–13 **KEY** VERSE

"My command is this: Love each other as I have loved you"
(John 15:12).

THE POINT

☞ **Real friends stick up for each other.**

THE BIBLE BASIS

Luke 19:1-10. Jesus visits Zacchaeus' home.

When Jesus came to town, Zacchaeus went along with the crowds to meet him. Zacchaeus climbed a sycamore tree to get a better vantage point—and possibly to avoid the jeers of the people around him. Because he was a tax collector, Zacchaeus was probably not well-liked. Tax collectors in Jesus' day often collected more than their fair share. But when Jesus saw Zacchaeus, he immediately invited himself to Zacchaeus' house for dinner. Zacchaeus felt honored that Jesus would choose him and promised to pay back all the money he'd stolen. Because Jesus saw the good in Zacchaeus, Zacchaeus changed his life.

By third and fourth grade, kids have established strong friendships. They're kind to their chosen friends but sometimes cruel to those they don't like. As a result, some kids may feel left out and put down, like Zacchaeus. But the memory of this feeling doesn't always last long. The next day, kids may band together with their friends to exclude someone else. Use this lesson to encourage kids to set aside their personal likes and dislikes to love and respect all people.

Other Scriptures used in this lesson are **Proverbs 18:24** and **Matthew 5:43-47.**

GETTING THE POINT

Students will

- see how quickly rumors can spread,
- learn how Jesus saw the good in people, and
- commit to sticking up for their friends.

THIS LESSON AT A GLANCE

Before the lesson, collect the necessary items from the Learning Lab for the activities you plan to use. Refer to the pictures in the margin to see what each item looks like.

SECTION	MINUTES	WHAT STUDENTS WILL DO	LEARNING LAB SUPPLIES	CLASSROOM SUPPLIES
ATTENTION GRABBER	up to 10	**ONE BIG BALL OF GOSSIP**—Make a big ball of clay to show how rumors are spread.	Clay	
BIBLE EXPLORATION AND APPLICATION	up to 15	**BEFORE AND AFTER**—Hear things people might have said about Zacchaeus and read Luke 19:1-10.	Cassette: "Zacchaeus"	Bibles, cassette player
	up to 18	**JESUS IS COMING TO DINNER**—Read Luke 19:1-6 and get the room ready for a visit from Jesus.	Metallic ribbons, paper streamer roll	Bibles, paper, markers, snacks, chalkboard and chalk or newsprint
	up to 12	**GIVE A GOOD WORD**—Discuss Matthew 5:43-47 and share positive comments about people they don't like.		Bibles, chalkboard and chalk or newsprint and marker
CLOSING	up to 5	**THE FRIENDSHIP CHAIN**—Read Proverbs 18:24 and make a chain to remind them to stick up for their friends.	Stacking clowns	Bible

Remember to make photocopies of the "Hands-On Fun at Home" handout (p. 126) to send home with your kids. The "Fun at Home" handout suggests ways for kids to talk with their families about what they're learning in class and helps them put their faith into action.

THE LESSON

As kids arrive, ask them which "Fun at Home" activities they tried. Ask questions such as "What did your family members say they're looking forward to in heaven?" and "Which Bible characters did you talk about meeting in heaven?"

Tell kids that whenever you ring the *gold foil bell*, they are to stop talking, raise their hands, and focus on you. Explain that it's important to respond to this signal quickly so the class can do as many fun activities as possible.

ATTENTION GRABBER

ONE BIG BALL OF GOSSIP
(up to 10 minutes)

LEARNING LAB

Form a circle and give each student a piece of *clay*. Say: **I want you to make up a silly story about me and spread it to others. I'll begin by telling a part of the story, then I'll pass my piece of *clay* to the person on my left. That person will add to the story and pass the *clay* again. I'll start by telling you that yesterday I woke up at my usual time. When the story comes to you, you might add something like, "Then she ate peanut butter soup for breakfast." Then add your piece of *clay* to mine and pass it to the person on your left. When everyone has added a piece to the story, the last person will share the whole story with the class.**

Have the last person give you the ball of *clay*. Then have that person tell the whole story. Ask:

● **Was the story we just heard a true story? Why or why not?** (Yes, because you really did get up on time; no, we all made things up to add to it.)

Say: **Stories that aren't always true but that people tell anyway are sometimes called rumors.**

● **How was our story like rumors people sometimes tell?** (Sometimes rumors start out to be true; people hear things, then they tell other people; people don't stop to think if something is true before they pass it on.)

● **What happens when people spread rumors?** (Sometimes the stories they tell aren't true; they might hurt people's feelings.)

Hold up the ball of *clay*. Say: **This ball started out as a little piece of clay. But as we added to the ball, it grew and grew, just like rumors sometimes grow. Rumors usually hurt people's feelings, and often they aren't even true. Real friends don't listen to rumors. ☞ Real friends stick up for each other no matter what other people say. Let's talk more today about what it takes to be a real friend.**

Return the *clay* to its container and place it out of sight.

TEACHER TIP

It's important to say The Point just as it's written in each activity. Repeating The Point over and over will help kids remember it and apply it to their lives.

 the POINT

BIBLE EXPLORATION AND APPLICATION

BEFORE AND AFTER
(up to 15 minutes)

Say: **Today we're going to hear a story about a man whose life was changed by his friendship with Jesus. We'll hear the things people might have said about this man before and after he met Jesus.**

Play the "Zacchaeus" segment of the *cassette tape.* After the first segment, stop the cassette player and ask:

● **How do you think Zacchaeus felt when he heard people grumbling about him?** (Upset; angry; sad.)

Form pairs. Distribute Bibles and have kids read the story of Zacchaeus from **Luke 19:1-10.** Encourage kids to take turns reading the verses.

After kids have finished reading, ring the *gold foil bell.* Wait for kids to respond, then restart the tape.

Stop the cassette player after the story and have kids discuss the following questions with partners. Pause after you ask each question to allow time for kids to discuss their answers. Ask:

● **How would you have felt if you had said bad things about Zacchaeus?** (Bad; silly; embarrassed.)

● **How do you react when you hear your friends grumbling about you?** (I get mad; I'm hurt; I feel like saying bad things about them.)

● **How do you react when your friends say encouraging things about you?** (I feel good; I'm happy; I feel like they're really my friends.)

● **What did Jesus say or do to encourage Zacchaeus?** (He told him to come down from the tree; he asked him to dinner.)

● **If Zacchaeus were your friend, how would you encourage him?** (By telling him he was a good person; by spending time with him.)

After about five minutes, call for kids' attention by ringing the *gold foil bell.* Wait for kids to respond, then invite pairs to share their insights with the rest of the class.

Say: **Even though Zacchaeus had done many wrong things, Jesus saw the good in him. Jesus didn't care what other people said about Zacchaeus because Jesus was a real friend. /☞ Real friends stick up for each other.**

BIBLE INSIGHT

Tax collectors were despised by the Jews because they collected money for the foreign powers that occupied Israel at that time. The collectors were also unliked because they were often unscrupulous and their work involved regular contact with the Gentiles, rendering them unclean.

the POINT ☞

JESUS IS COMING TO DINNER
(up to 18 minutes)

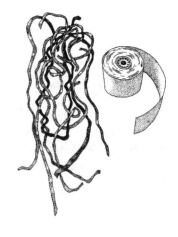

Before class, gather ingredients for snacks that kids can help prepare, such as cheese and crackers or peanut butter and celery sticks.

Say: **Zacchaeus must have been surprised when Jesus spoke to him.** Ask a volunteer to read **Luke 19:1-6** aloud. Then say: **Imagine that Jesus just told us he is coming *here*, to our classroom, in 10 minutes!** Ask:

● **How are we going to get the room ready?** (Clean up; decorate; get some food.)

Form three groups. Have one group straighten up the room and arrange the furniture as if for a dinner party. Give the second group a handful of *metallic ribbons*, several 2- to 3-foot pieces of the *paper streamer roll*, paper, markers, and tape. Have them decorate the room and make a banner welcoming Jesus. Have the third group prepare the food.

While kids are getting the room ready, write the following questions on a chalkboard or a sheet of newsprint taped to a wall. After 10 minutes, ring the *gold foil bell.* Wait for kids to respond, then have them sit in the area prepared by group 1. Ask group 3 to serve the food. Be sure to compliment group 2 on the decorations. As kids are eating, discuss these questions:

● **What other ways could we make Jesus feel welcome in our room?** (Read the Bible; offer him a chair; talk to him.)

● **If Jesus were sitting next to you, what would you say to him?** (I'd thank him for loving me; I'd ask him what heaven was like.)

● **What do you think Zacchaeus learned from his meeting with Jesus?** (To look for the good in people; that Jesus was a true friend.)

● **What would you do if you found out Jesus was coming to your house tomorrow?** (Clean up my room; be nice to my sister; read my Bible; pray.)

● **Even though we can't see Jesus, he's always with us. He wants to be part of our lives. How can we welcome Jesus into our lives?** (By doing what Jesus wants us to do; by showing love; by being a good friend.)

Say: **Zacchaeus didn't expect Jesus to come to his house, but meeting Jesus was the best thing that ever happened to him. Jesus was a real friend to Zacchaeus, even though Zacchaeus wasn't too popular with other people. We can be real friends, too. We can welcome Jesus by following his example and being a friend to other people.** ☞ **Real friends stick up for each other.**

Collect the *paper streamer roll* and *metallic ribbons* for use in future lessons. Have kids help you clean up any leftover food.

☜ the POINT

KEY VERSE
CONNECTION

"My command is this: Love each other as I have loved you" (John 15:12).

Third- and fourth-graders are still learning about what being and having true friends really means. Teach them that when they are confused about what friendship is, they can look to Jesus as an example of the greatest friend they'll ever have.

Say: **Even though other people thought Zacchaeus wasn't very nice, Jesus still loved him and wanted to be his friend. Jesus wants us to treat everyone with love and respect, even people we don't really like. Let's read what Jesus says about this in the Bible.**

Form trios. Distribute Bibles and have kids look up **Matthew 5:43-47.** Have each trio pick a reader to read the verses, an interpreter to summarize the verses in his or her own words, and an encourager to make sure everyone gets a turn to respond to discussion questions about the verses.

While kids are reading the verses, write the following questions on a chalkboard or a sheet of newsprint taped to a wall. When kids have finished reading, ring the *gold foil bell.* Wait for kids to respond, then have them discuss the following questions in their trios. Remind the encourager to help everyone participate. Ask:

● **Why is it so easy to love your friends?** (Because they like to do the things I like to do; because they're nice to me.)

● **Why is it hard to love your enemies?** (Because they're mean to me; because I don't like them.)

● **What do you think would happen if you started being nice to your enemies and praying for them?** (They might be nice to me; God would help me not to hate them.)

After several minutes, ring the *gold foil bell.* Wait for kids to respond, then invite partners to share their responses with the rest of the class. Say: **It's natural to like some people more than others. The people we like best usually become our friends. It's easy to show love and respect to our friends. But it's not so easy to show love and respect to people we don't like. We're going to practice that now. Don't say anything out loud, but think of a person at school you don't really like. Then in your trios, take turns filling in this sentence without mentioning the person's name: "I'm thinking of someone it's hard for me to like because..." You'll have about two minutes. Go.**

After two minutes, ring the *gold foil bell.* Wait for kids to respond, then say: **With the same person in mind, take turns filling in this sentence: "Some things I could learn to like about that person are..."**

After two minutes, ring the *gold foil bell.* Wait for kids to respond, then say: **With the same person in mind, take turns filling in one more sentence: "One thing I could do to show love to that person is..."**

After two minutes, ring the *gold foil bell.* Wait for kids to respond, then ask:

● **Was it easy or hard to think of things you could learn to like about that person? Explain.** (Hard, because I kept thinking of all the reasons I didn't like him; easy, because I just thought of the things I like about my friends.)

● **Why is it important to treat other people with love and respect?** (That's what Jesus would do; that's the way I'd want to be treated.)

Say: **It's really hard to see good things in people we don't like,** but that's what Jesus wants us to do. Everyone thought that Zacchaeus was mean and rotten, but Jesus saw that he could change. Sometimes if we stick up for people we don't really like, we discover they're not so bad after all. We might even want them to become our friends.  Real friends stick up for each other.

Hands-On FUN AT HOME

We believe that Christian education extends beyond the classroom into the home. Photocopy the "Hands-On Fun at Home" handout (p. 126) for this week and send it home with your kids. Encourage kids to try several activities and discuss the Bible verses and questions with their parents.

CLOSING

THE FRIENDSHIP CHAIN
(up to 5 minutes)

Have kids sit in a circle, and give each person a *stacking clown*. If you have more than 10 students in your class, form two circles for this activity. Say: **The Bible talks about real friends. Listen.** Read **Proverbs 18:24** aloud, then say:  **Real friends stick up for each other. Jesus was a real friend to Zacchaeus, and we can be real friends to one another. To remind us to be real friends, let's join our *stacking clowns* to create a friendship chain. When the chain comes to you, say one way you can be a better friend and add your *stacking clown* to the friendship chain—then pass the chain to the person on your left.**

As the chain gets longer, it will eventually break. If your chain breaks, point out to kids that friendships are fragile, just like the chain. Then have the next person put the chain back together before adding his or her *stacking clown*.

When you've completed your friendship chain, collect the *stacking clowns* for use in future lessons. If no one else uses your room, leave the chain assembled and hang it on a wall or bulletin board. Close with prayer, asking God to help kids stick up for their friends this week.

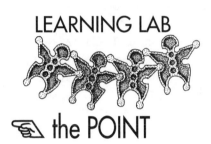

LEARNING LAB

the POINT

Hands-On FUN! AT HOME

LESSON 10: STICKING TOGETHER

the POINT ☞ **Real friends stick up for each other.**

■ ■ ■ ■ ■ ■ ■ ■ ■ ■ ■ ■ ■ ■

"My command is this: Love each other as I have loved you" (John 15:12).

BIBLE FOCUS

CHECK it OUT

Read 1 Samuel 20:1-42.
What made Jonathan a good friend? How can you be a friend like Jonathan?

Read Proverbs 17:17.
How can you help your friends in times of trouble?

"STICK 'EM UP" prayers

Ask your parents to get you a pad of self-stick notes. On each note, write the name of one friend and one way you can stick up for that friend this week. Each day, stick one of your notes to your dresser or mirror to remind you to pray for that friend. When you pray, ask God to give you the courage to stick up for your friend.

FAITH walk

One night at dinner this week, ask your parents about the childhood friends they had when they were your age. Ask them who their best friends were and what they did together. Did they help their friends through any tough times? Are they still friends today? Why or why not?

STICK-TOGETHER SNACK

Make this simple snack anytime you want a nutritious pick-me-up. Spread peanut butter on two pieces of bread, then add a sliced banana to one piece. Top with the other piece and enjoy! As you savor your snack, think about how friends stick together just like the peanut butter sticks your sandwich together.

LESSON 11

REACHING OUT

for Lessons 10–13 **KEY** VERSE

"My command is this: Love each other as I have loved you" (John 15:12).

THE POINT

☞ **Real friends comfort each other when they're sad.**

THE BIBLE BASIS

Mark 6:45-51. Jesus comforts his disciples during a storm.

Jesus told his disciples to get into their boat and go ahead of him to the other side of the lake. As they were rowing, a storm blew in. Suddenly, they found themselves rowing through raging waves and howling winds. As rowing became more and more difficult, they became increasingly frightened about what might happen to them. To their amazement, they saw a figure walking toward them on top of the water. At first they thought it was a ghost, but then they heard the voice of Jesus, telling them not to be frightened. When Jesus got into the boat, the storm immediately stopped. The sea became quiet and peaceful again. The disciples were amazed at what Jesus had done, and they were comforted by his presence.

By third and fourth grade, kids have abandoned many of their childhood fears. They're no longer afraid of the dark—at least, they don't want to admit that fear. Eight- and 9-year-olds are afraid of bigger things such as having to leave their friends or losing a parent through death or divorce. Some kids may seem fearless, but few really are. And all kids, whether they realize it or not, have friends for whom these fears are all too real. This lesson will teach kids that Jesus is a friend who stands ready to comfort them, just as he comforted his disciples in the storm. Kids will also learn to comfort their friends who feel sad or afraid.

Other Scriptures used in this lesson are **Psalm 118:5-6** and **2 Corinthians 7:4.**

GETTING THE POINT

Students will
- identify times they're sad or afraid,
- practice comforting each other, and
- commit to relying on Jesus to comfort them.

THIS LESSON AT A GLANCE

Before the lesson, collect the necessary items from the Learning Lab for the activities you plan to use. Refer to the pictures in the margin to see what each item looks like.

SECTION	MINUTES	WHAT STUDENTS WILL DO	LEARNING LAB SUPPLIES	CLASSROOM SUPPLIES
ATTENTION GRABBER	up to 12	**MAKE ME LAUGH!**—Practice comforting each other by making each other laugh.	Cassette: "Make Me Laugh," pine cone, shape puzzle, chef's hat, top pen, stacking clowns, multicolored feathers, gold foil bell	Cassette player, paper sack
BIBLE EXPLORATION AND APPLICATION	up to 12	**STORM AT SEA**—Hear about a time Jesus comforted his disciples.	Cassette: "Storm at Sea"	Bible, cassette player, "Story at Sea" handouts (p. 135)
	up to 15	**BLUES, BLUES, BLUES**—Brainstorm situations in which they feel sad or afraid and read Psalm 118:5-6.	Pine cone	Bibles, chalkboard and chalk or newsprint and marker, tape
	up to 15	**FRIENDLY COMFORT**—Practice comforting one another and read 2 Corinthians 7:4.	Multicolored feathers	Bible, tape, pencils, index cards
CLOSING	up to 6	**A POWERFUL FRIEND**—Affirm the calming effect of Jesus' presence.	Accordion flower	

Remember to make photocopies of the "Hands-On Fun at Home" handout (p. 136) to send home with your kids. The "Fun at Home" handout suggests ways for kids to talk with their families about what they're learning in class and helps them put their faith into action.

THE LESSON

As kids arrive, ask them which "Fun at Home" activities they tried. Ask questions such as "How did you stick up for your friends last week?" and "What are some ways you or your family showed friendship recently?"

Tell kids that whenever you ring the *gold foil bell,* they are to stop talking, raise their hands, and focus on you. Explain that it's important to respond to this signal quickly so the class can do as many fun activities as possible.

ATTENTION GRABBER

MAKE ME LAUGH!
(up to 12 minutes)

LEARNING LAB

Before class, put one *pine cone,* one *shape puzzle,* the *chef's hat,* one *top pen,* five *stacking clowns,* and 10 *multicolored feathers* in a paper sack.

Form trios. Say: **We're going to play a game based on an old TV game show called *Make Me Laugh!* The object of the game is to make another person laugh by making silly faces, telling funny jokes, or doing funny actions. Tickling is not allowed.**

In your group, decide who will be the comedian, who will be the contestant, and who will be the judge. We'll play the game three times so everyone gets a chance to try all three roles.

Pause to let kids choose their roles. Ring the *gold foil bell* to regain their attention. Wait for kids to respond, then continue: **If you're the contestant, your job is to keep from laughing. If you're the comedian, your job is to make the contestant laugh. You'll have 30 seconds, and you'll be allowed to pick one item from the "grab bag" to help you. If you're the judge, your job is to decide when and if the contestant laughs. You can start when you hear the *gold foil bell.***

Let each comedian draw from the grab bag, then ring the *gold foil bell.* Play the first part of the "Make Me Laugh" segment of the *cassette tape.* Stop the cassette player after you hear the buzzer. Have kids switch roles and repeat the game twice so each person gets a chance to play each role. Play the "Make Me Laugh" segment each time.

After kids have completed the third round, ring the *gold foil bell.* Wait for kids to respond, then ask:

● **Was it easy or hard to make your friends laugh? Explain.** (Easy, because I grabbed something funny from the bag; hard, because I couldn't think of anything funny to do.)

TEACHER TIP

Some kids may not want to try all three roles. If all three group members are satisfied with the first roles they chose, let them repeat the same roles each time.

● **Can you tell about a time someone made you laugh when you were feeling sad? Explain.** (My sister told me a silly joke; my best friend leaned down from the top bunk and made a funny face.)

Say: **Making people laugh is a good way to comfort them when they're feeling sad. Today we're going to talk about ways we can comfort our friends. We'll learn that** **real friends comfort each other when they're sad or afraid.**

Retrieve the Learning Lab items for use in future lessons.

the POINT

LEARNING LAB

FOLDED UP

FOLDED DOWN

BIBLE EXPLORATION AND APPLICATION

STORM AT SEA
(up to 12 minutes)

Before class, make copies of the "Story at Sea" handout (p. 135). The handout will look like a collection of lines and squiggles at first. But when it's folded correctly, two distinct pictures will emerge. One picture will show a boat on a stormy sea. The other picture will show Jesus comforting the disciples on a calm sea.

Practice folding the handout before you distribute copies to the kids. Fold the solid lines so the creases face you. Fold the dotted lines so the creases face away from you. When you've completed all the folds, push the creases facing you toward the top of the page to reveal the first picture. Push the creases toward the bottom of the page to reveal the second picture. Both pictures are shown in the margin. Bring your folded handout with you to class, but don't let kids see it until they've completed their folds.

Distribute copies of the "Story at Sea" handout to the kids. Open your Bible to **Mark 6:45-51** and show kids the passage. Say: **We're going to hear a Bible story now about a time Jesus comforted his disciples. While we're listening, we're going to make pictures of the story appear by folding our handouts. Fold the solid lines upward and the dotted lines inward to make your pictures appear.**

Demonstrate an upward and an inward fold, then continue: **When you've finished folding, push your folds in one direction to see a picture of part of the story. Then push them in the other direction to see a picture of another part of the story. Remember to be quiet and listen as you're folding. If you need help, raise your hand.**

Play the "Storm at Sea" segment of the *cassette tape*. As kids are folding their handouts, circulate among the kids to offer help as necessary.

After you've stopped the cassette player, help students who haven't finished folding their handouts. Then ask:

● **What would you think if, like the disciples, you saw Jesus walking on the water?** (I wouldn't believe it; I'd be scared; I'd feel relieved when I found out it was Jesus.)

● **How did Jesus calm his friends' fears?** (By letting them know he wasn't a ghost; he told them not to be afraid.)

● **How can you let Jesus calm your fears?** (By trusting him; by praying about the things that scare me.)

Hold up the folded handout you brought to class and push the folds so the stormy sea is showing. Have kids push their folds the same way. Say: **Sometimes life looks really scary. But if we look to Jesus for help, he can calm our fears.**

Push the folds of your handout the other way to show Jesus comforting his disciples. Have kids push their folds the same way. Say: **Jesus is the best friend anyone can have. He was there to comfort his friends when they faced a scary situation, and he's always ready to comfort us, too.** ☞ **Real friends comfort you when you're sad or afraid.**

 BLUES, BLUES, BLUES
(up to 15 minutes)

Say: **The storm at sea was definitely a scary situation for Jesus' disciples. Let's think about what makes us afraid or sad. I'm going to pass around the *pine cone*. When it comes to you, tell us something that makes you sad or afraid, then break off a "cold prickly" from the *pine cone*. Set your cold prickly on the floor in front of you until I give you more directions.**

Start by giving an example of your own. If kids don't want to share a fear, encourage them to share something that makes them feel sad or upset.

Write kids' responses on a chalkboard or newsprint taped to a wall. When the *pine cone* comes back to you, place it out of sight. Give each person a piece of tape, then say: **Tape your cold prickly to your hand. Then find a partner and talk about the following questions.** Pause after you ask each question to allow kids time for discussion. Ask:

● **Which one of these situations makes you feel most sad or afraid? Why?** (Having a pet die makes me sad because I miss having it around; moving to a new place makes me afraid because I don't know if I'll make new friends.)

● **How is having the cold prickly taped to your hand like being in that situation?** (The cold prickly doesn't feel good, and I don't feel good when those things happen to me; sometimes sad feelings stick with me for a long time.)

After pairs have had time to discuss the questions, ring the *gold foil bell*. Wait for kids to respond, then distribute Bibles. Say: **The Bible tells us what we can do when we're afraid. I'll show you where to look.** Have kids find **Psalm 118:5-6.** Ask a volunteer to read the verse.

Say: ☞ **Real friends comfort you when you're sad or afraid. Praying together is a great way for friends to comfort each other. The verses we just read are one of the psalmist's prayers of thanks-**

 **the POINT**

LEARNING LAB

 **the POINT**

the POINT

LEARNING LAB

giving. **Pray that prayer with your partner. Take turns reading the verses aloud. When you get to the part in verse 6 that says, "I will not be afraid," change the sentence by adding one of the scary situations we talked about. For example, you might pray, "I will not be afraid of being alone, because the Lord is with me."**

After kids have finished praying with their partners, close the prayer time by saying something like **"Thank you, God, for comforting us when we're sad or afraid. In Jesus' name, amen."**

FRIENDLY COMFORT
(up to 15 minutes)

Have kids remain in their pairs. Distribute *multicolored feathers*, index cards, tape, and pencils. Say: **Real friends comfort each other when they're sad or afraid. Sometimes it's hard to know the right things to say to comfort people. We're going to practice comforting each other now so that when our friends are really scared, we'll know what to do.**

On one side of your index card, write about a time you felt sad or afraid. It could be the situation you shared earlier, or it could be something else you want to share with your partner but didn't want to tell the whole class.

After about one minute, ring the *gold foil bell*. Wait for kids to respond, then say: **Now trade cards with your partner. Read your partner's situation, then write a note or draw a picture on the other side of the card that would comfort your partner in that situation.**

After two or three minutes, ring the *gold foil bell*. Wait for kids to respond, then say: **If you're the younger partner, take the cold prickly off your partner's hand and tape it to the side of your partner's card with the scary situation written on it. Then put your feather over the spot on your partner's hand where the cold prickly was and read how you would comfort your partner in that situation.** If you didn't do the previous activity with the cold pricklies, simply have children put the feathers on their partners' hands as they read their cards. **When the younger partners finish, older partners will do the same thing.**

After about five minutes, ring the *gold foil bell*. Invite volunteers to share ways they'd comfort their partners. Then ask:

● **What was it like when your partner took off your cold prickly?** (Better—my hand didn't hurt anymore; I felt like my partner cared about me.)

● **How did the touch of the feather feel to your hand?** (Soft; nice; it kind of tickled.)

● **How was the feeling of the feather like the way you feel when someone comforts you?** (The softness of the feather made me forget about the cold prickly, and when someone comforts me I forget about what was making me sad; the feather felt nice, and it's nice when people care about me.)

● **Was it easy or hard for you to think of a way to comfort your partner? Explain.** (Easy, because I'm friends with my partner and I know what she likes; hard, because I wanted to make him laugh, but I didn't want him to think I was laughing at the thing that scared him.)

● **What is it like when someone tries to comfort you when you're scared or sad about something in real life?** (Good; I'm glad to know that they care; sometimes it doesn't help.)

Say: **In the Bible, Paul told his friends how he felt about them. Let's see what he said.** Read **2 Corinthians 7:4.** Say: **We've thought of a lot of good ways to comfort our friends today. Let's use the words of this verse to thank our partners for comforting us. If** (name of student) **were my partner, I'd say, "**(Name of student)**, I feel very sure of you and am very proud of you. You give me comfort." After you thank your partner, tape your feather to the comfort side of your card as a reminder of how nice it feels to be comforted.**

After about two minutes, ring the *gold foil bell.* Wait for kids to respond, then say: **The times we need comfort are the times we need our friends the most. When you need comfort, you can count on your friends in this class.**  **Real friends comfort each other when they're sad or afraid.**

Hands-On FUN AT HOME
We believe that Christian education extends beyond the classroom into the home. Photocopy the "Hands-On Fun at Home" handout (p. 136) for this week and send it home with your kids. Encourage kids to try several activities and discuss the Bible verses and questions with their parents.

the POINT

CLOSING

A POWERFUL FRIEND
(up to 6 minutes)

Have kids form a circle. Hold up the unopened *accordion flower* and say: **If I don't open this flower, it's just a bunch of tissue paper glued between two plastic sticks. But when I open the flower** (snap open the *accordion flower*)**, it cheers me up with its bright colors. The bright colors are always there, but I have to reach for the flower and open it in order to see them. Jesus is always there for us, too. He's a real friend, who's always ready to comfort us if we ask him to.**  **Real friends comfort each other when they're sad or afraid.**

I'm going to pass the flower around and let each of you snap it open. But before you open it, repeat this prayer: "Jesus, thank you for loving and comforting me."

LEARNING LAB

the POINT

When the *accordion flower* comes back to you, return it to the Learning Lab. Encourage kids to take home their comfort cards and look at them when they're feeling sad or afraid this week.

Story at Sea

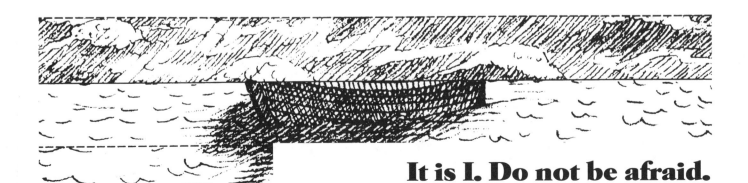

It is I. Do not be afraid.

Hands-On FUN AT HOME

LESSON 11:
REACHING OUT

the POINT ☞ **Real friends comfort each other when they're sad or afraid.**

■ ■ ■ ■ ■ ■ ■ ■ ■ ■ ■ ■ ■

"My command is this: Love each other as I have loved you" (John 15:12).

BIBLE FOCUS

NOTABLES

Cut out the certificate below and present it to a friend or family member when that person needs comfort.

Dear _____,

This certificate entitles you to

one free hour of the comfort of your choice

the next time you feel sad or afraid.

Your friend, _____

FAITH walk

Designate a chair in your living or family room as the "comfort chair" for a week. Put a sign on it and invite family members to sit in the chair when they've had a sad or disappointing day. When you see someone sitting in the chair, gather the rest of the family for a quick comfort session. You might bring the person's favorite food or a bouquet of flowers or just sit and talk. Be sure to smile a lot!

CHECK it OUT

Read Luke 10:25-37.
The Samaritan gave aid and comfort to a man who was supposed to be his enemy. What would you do if someone you didn't like needed comfort?

Read Psalm 23.
How can you let God comfort you when you're sad or afraid?

COMFORT cookies

Create these Scripture fortune cookies to comfort your family and friends. On slips of paper, write Bible verses of comfort such as 2 Corinthians 1:4; Matthew 5:4; and John 14:27.

Beat 4 egg whites with 1 cup sugar. Add ½ cup flour, ¼ teaspoon salt, ½ teaspoon vanilla, and 2 tablespoons water. Blend in ½ cup

melted butter. Pour batter in 3-inch circles on a heavily greased cookie sheet. Bake at 375° for

about 8 minutes. While the cookies are still warm, fold the circles into fortune cookies—with a Scripture strip inside each one.

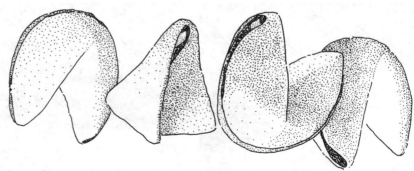

LESSON 12

POSITIVE PEERS

for Lessons 10–13 **KEY** *VERSE*

"My command is this: Love each other as I have loved you" (John 15:12).

THE POINT

☞ **Real friends don't ask you to do things that are wrong.**

THE BIBLE BASIS

John 15:12-17. Jesus calls his disciples his friends.

Being a friend of Jesus probably wasn't easy. Everywhere Jesus went, people whispered, pointed, and speculated about who he was and what he was doing. Jesus encouraged his disciples to remain faithful by reminding them that they weren't just his servants, they were his friends. Because of their friendship with Jesus, they could expect God to grant the requests they made in Jesus' name. In the verses that follow John 15:12-17, Jesus warned his friends to maintain their friendship with him even though the world might persecute them.

Third- and fourth-graders are just beginning to experience significant peer pressure. They may be pressured to share answers on tests or homework, use swear words, or put others down. Although peer pressure will increase and intensify as kids grow older, third grade isn't too early to learn to identify and resist negative peer pressure. This lesson also addresses the importance of positive peer pressure. It encourages students to rely on other Christian friends to help them do what's right and maintain their friendship with Jesus.

Other Scriptures used in this lesson are **Proverbs 18:24; 1 Corinthians 10:13; 15:33;** and **Philippians 4:13.**

GETTING THE POINT

Students will
- evaluate the importance of friends' opinions,
- practice ways to resist negative peer pressure, and
- encourage one another to follow Jesus.

THIS LESSON AT A GLANCE

Before the lesson, collect the necessary items from the Learning Lab for the activities you plan to use. Refer to the pictures in the margin to see what each item looks like.

SECTION	MINUTES	WHAT STUDENTS WILL DO	LEARNING LAB SUPPLIES	CLASSROOM SUPPLIES
ATTENTION GRABBER	up to 5	**PULL TOGETHER**—Link arms and try to pick up neon loops in each corner of the room.	Neon loops	Markers, paper, tape
BIBLE EXPLORATION AND APPLICATION	up to 15	**PRESSURE MEASURE**—Make a human scale to measure pressure situations and read Proverbs 18:24 and 1 Corinthians 15:33.		Bibles, masking tape
	up to 20	**GET ME OUTTA HERE**—Discuss 1 Corinthians 10:13 and practice ways to resist negative peer pressure.		Bible, index cards, "Escape Hatch" handouts (p. 145), pencils
	up to 15	**POSITIVE PRESSURE**—Contrast negative and positive peer pressure and read John 15:12-14.	Gold foil bell	Bibles
CLOSING	up to 5	**CIRCLE OF STRENGTH**—Read Philippians 4:13 and commit to help one another stand up for what's right.		Bible

Remember to make photocopies of the "Hands-On Fun at Home" handout (p. 146) to send home with your kids. The "Fun at Home" handout suggests ways for kids to talk with their families about what they're learning in class and helps them put their faith into action.

THE LESSON

As kids arrive, ask them which "Fun at Home" activities they tried last week. Ask questions such as "How did you comfort someone in your family recently?" and "How were you comforted by someone else?"

Tell kids that whenever you ring the *gold foil bell,* they are to stop talking, raise their hands, and focus on you. Explain that it's important to respond to this signal quickly so the class can do as many fun activities as possible. Practice the signal two or three times.

ATTENTION GRABBER

PULL TOGETHER
(up to 5 minutes)

LEARNING LAB

Before class, label the four corners of the room from 1 to 4. In each corner, put one *neon loop* for every four students in your class.

Form groups of no more than four. Have group members number off from 1 to 4, then say: **In your groups, stand in a circle facing outward, then link elbows.**

Pause to allow students to link elbows, then continue: **I've placed several *neon loops* in each corner of the room. There will be one *neon loop* for each group in all four corners. When I say "go," you'll have five minutes to collect all the *neon loops* for your group. You must stay in your circle formation the whole time. When you're within an arm's length of the corner, one person may reach out and grab a *neon loop*. Ones, try to lead your group to corner #1. Twos, try to lead your group to corner #2. Threes, try to lead your group to corner #3. Fours, try to lead your group to corner #4. Ready, go!**

After five minutes, call for kids' attention by ringing the *gold foil bell.* Wait for kids to respond, then applaud the teams that managed to collect all their *neon loops.* Gather all the *neon loops,* then ask:

● **Was it easy or hard to collect all the *neon loops*? Why?** (Easy, because we all agreed to take turns pulling each other; hard, because we were all trying to go in separate directions.)

● **What was it like to try to collect the *neon loop* in your corner while your teammates were trying to collect the *neon loops* from other corners?** (Frustrating; impossible; I felt like I was being pulled apart.)

● **How was being pushed and pulled by your teammates in this game like being pressured by your friends in real life?** (Sometimes I want to do one thing, but my friends want to do something else; sometimes I get talked into doing things I really don't want to do.)

Say: **Often our friends try to pull us toward the things they want to do, just like you tried to pull your group toward your corner.**

the POINT

Today we'll be learning about ways friends can influence each other. Our friends can tempt us to do things that are wrong or encourage us to do what's right. Real friends are encouragers. Real friends don't ask you to do things that are wrong.

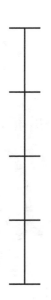

BIBLE EXPLORATION AND APPLICATION

PRESSURE MEASURE
(up to 15 minutes)

Before class, stick a 10-foot strip of masking tape to the floor across the center of your classroom. Use tape to divide the line into four equal segments, as shown in the margin diagram.

Stand at one end of the line and say: **Let's see why our friends have such a big influence on us. I'm going to read some statements. If you really agree with my statement, stand at the end of the line by me. If you really disagree, stand at the other end of the line. If you sort of agree, stand closer to my end. If you sort of disagree, stand closer to the other end. If you're not sure, stand somewhere in the middle.**

Read the following statements one at a time, pausing after each statement to allow kids to indicate their opinions by their positions on the line.

- **I don't care what people think of me.**
- **I don't care what my friends think of me.**
- **I want my best friends to like me.**
- **I want everyone to like me.**

Let kids remain in their most recent positions as you ask:

- **Why do we care what other people think of us?** (Because if they don't like me, I won't have any friends; I know I'm a good person whether others like me or not.)

Continue reading the following statements:

- **I want my friends to like the clothes I wear.**
- **I want my friends to like the activities I choose.**
- **I'm willing to try new things to make friends.**
- **I'm willing to do anything to make friends.**

Have kids stand still as you ask:

- **Think about the spot where you're standing; how much influence do your friends have on the choices you make? Why?** (A lot, because we like the same things; not much, because I usually make my friends try the things I like to do.)

Have kids sit down in their spots on the tape line. Distribute Bibles, then say: **If you're sitting on the "agree" side of the line, go to corner #1. If you're sitting on the "disagree" side of the line, go to corner #3. We'll see what the Bible has to say about friends.**

TEACHER TIP

If you don't have time to tape a line on the floor, designate an imaginary line and mark the ends with two chairs.

Have the kids in corner #1 look up **Proverbs 18:24** and read it with a partner. Have the kids in corner #3 look up **1 Corinthians 15:33** and read it with a partner.

After several minutes, ring the *gold foil bell.* Wait for kids to respond, then say: **Find a partner from the other corner and tell that person about the verse you read. Then I'll ask some questions for you and your partner to discuss.**

Allow one or two minutes for partners to share their verses, then ask the following questions. Pause after each question to allow kids time for discussion. Ask:

● **What harmful things might your friends encourage you to do?** (Drink; do drugs; put other people down; skip class to play outside.)

● **What can you learn from these verses that might help you choose real friends?** (Choose friends who are Christians; don't choose friends who will get me in trouble.)

After kids have finished discussing the questions, ring the *gold foil bell.* Wait for kids to respond, then invite them to share the responses they discussed with their partners.

Say: **It's natural to want to fit in with a crowd of friends. That's why it's important to choose our friends carefully, because friends can be powerful influences on us. Real friends can help us do what's right, even when the right thing may not be the most popular. Real friends don't ask you to do things that are wrong.**

GET ME OUTTA HERE
(up to 20 minutes)

Say: **Many of you may have heard the expression "Just say no." When you're feeling pressured to do something you don't want to do, saying no is a good way to get out of that situation. But it's not always easy to say no. Today we're going to practice some specific ways to get out of situations where we feel pressured. Then, when we're really in those situations, we'll know how to say no.**

Form groups of no more than four and give each group an index card and a pencil. Have each group choose a recorder to write down the group's pressure situation, an encourager to make sure everyone participates in the discussion, a timekeeper to make sure the group finishes on time, and a delivery person to deliver the group's situation to the teacher.

Say: **In your groups, think of a time when you might feel pressured to do something that's wrong. Maybe your friend wants you to come out to play even though you haven't done your chores, or a classmate wants to copy your math homework. Try to pick a situation everyone agrees on. When you've agreed on a situation, write that situation down on your card and have your delivery person bring it to me. Timekeepers, keep an eye on the clock. You'll have only two minutes to do this.**

As kids are working, circulate among the groups to offer ideas. After

TEACHER TIP
If most of your kids are on one side of the line, redistribute the groups so an equal number of kids goes to each corner.

the POINT

KEY VERSE
CONNECTION

"My command is this: Love each other as I have loved you" (John 15:12).

God doesn't want us to love only the people who do the right things. Use the Key Verse to help kids understand that "Just say no" doesn't mean "Just say hate," and Jesus' command to love each other applies to our enemies as well as our friends.

two minutes, ring the *gold foil bell*. Wait for kids to respond, then collect any remaining cards from the delivery people. Shuffle the cards, then redistribute them. Make sure groups don't receive their own cards. Distribute copies of the "Escape Hatch" handout (p. 145) to each group.

Say: **God will never leave us in a pressure situation without a way out.** Read **1 Corinthians 10:13** aloud. **Take a moment to look at the responses on your "Escape Hatch" handout.**

Give kids a moment to look over the handout, then continue: **Practice using those responses to get out of the pressure situation written on your group's card. Have one person in your group try to resist while the rest of your group tries to pressure that person. If you're the person being pressured, choose the response you like best and see how it works. Then trade cards with another group and let another person try to resist.**

Circulate among the groups to offer help and ideas. Encourage the "pressurers" to say things like "Come on, everybody's doing it," "Your parents won't find out," or "If you won't do it, I'll find another friend who will." Remind the pressurers to go along with the responses on the handout. For example, if the "pressuree" changes the subject, they should follow the change. If pressurees seem to be stumped, suggest they try another response.

After kids have all had a chance to practice resisting, ring the *gold foil bell*. Wait for kids to respond, then ask:

● **What was your reaction when your friends tried to pressure you?** (I was frustrated; I was nervous; it was OK, because I knew they didn't really mean it.)

● **Which responses worked best for you as you tried to resist the pressure? Why?** (Changing the subject, because they were more interested in sports than in pressuring me; acting shocked, because that made them realize they were asking me to do something wrong.)

● **Did having a response ready help you? Why or why not?** (Yes, because I usually give in if I don't know what to say; no, they just kept pressuring me anyway.)

Say: **If someone tries to pressure you to do something that's wrong, you should wonder if that person is really a friend after all.**  **Real friends don't ask you to do things that are wrong. The next time someone asks you to do something you think is wrong, try one of the responses you practiced today and ask God to show you the way out.**

the POINT

LEARNING LAB

POSITIVE PRESSURE
(up to 15 minutes)

Ask two volunteers to leave the room and stand just outside the door. Form two groups from the remaining students by assigning students with birthdays from January to June to one group and students with birthdays from July to December to the other group. Say: **When our volunteers** come back into the room, we're going to help them find two objects. The first object, a Bible, will represent encouragement to do what's right. Where should we hide the Bible?

Quickly decide where to hide the Bible, then continue: **The second object is the *gold foil bell*. Often we hear a bell or a buzzer as a warning when something's about to go wrong. The *gold foil bell* will represent the pressure to do what's wrong. Let's hide the *gold foil bell* on the opposite side of the room from the Bible. Where should we hide it?**

Quickly decide where to hide the bell. Then say: **When our volunteers come back, the January-to-June group will give the volunteers directions to find the Bible, and the July-to-December group will give the volunteers directions to find the *gold foil bell*. Give directions by saying "cold" if the volunteers are far from your object, "warm" if they're headed in the right direction, and "hot" if they're really close to it. You'll need to remember to use inside voices when you're giving your directions. Since we've hidden the *gold foil bell*, I'll flash the lights three times when I want you to stop giving directions.**

Assign one of the objects to each group, then bring back the two volunteers. Say: (Names of volunteers), **we've hidden something somewhere in this room. In a moment, we'll help you find the object we've hidden. You'll have two minutes to work together to find it.**

Signal the kids to begin giving "hotter" and "colder" directions. After two minutes, flash the lights three times. Wait for kids to respond, then reveal the hidden objects if the volunteers didn't find them. Hold up the Bible and the *gold foil bell*. Say: **The Bible represented encouragement to do what's right, and the bell represented pressure to do things that are wrong.** Ask:

● **Volunteers, what was it like to try to follow our directions?** (Confusing, because one group pointed me one way and the other group pointed in the opposite direction; frustrating; after a while I felt like giving up.)

● **How did you decide who to listen to?** (I listened to my friends; I followed the loudest directions.)

● **Group members, what was it like trying to get the volunteers to follow your directions instead of the other group's?** (Hard, because they couldn't hear us; frustrating, because we couldn't tell them what they were looking for.)

● **What could we have done differently to make it easier for our volunteers to find the hidden objects?** (Given only one set of directions; told them what they were looking for.)

● **How was this activity like the pressure you feel when different people try to influence your decisions?** (Sometimes it's hard to know who to listen to; sometimes I give in if people keep trying to convince me.)

BIBLE *INSIGHT*

Even though the Gospel of John has biographical basis, it is not organized in a strictly chronological order, as are the other three Gospels. John's main intention was to emphasize the creation of a relationship and to involve the reader actively in his or her belief in Jesus as the Christ.

the POINT

Say: **Jesus knew how to be a real friend.** Distribute Bibles and have kids look up **John 15:12-14.** When everyone has found the passage, ask a volunteer to read it.

Say: **Real friends don't ask you to do things that are wrong. Real friends *do* help you do what's right. One of the best ways we can show love for our friends is by encouraging them to follow Jesus and do what he wants us to do. Jesus wants us to be his friends. And Jesus is the best friend we could possibly have.**

Hands-On FUN AT HOME

We believe that Christian education extends beyond the classroom into the home. Photocopy the "Hands-On Fun at Home" handout (p. 146) for this week and send it home with your kids. Encourage kids to try several activities and discuss the Bible verses and questions with their parents.

CLOSING

CIRCLE OF STRENGTH
(up to 5 minutes)

Open your Bible to **Philippians 4:13.** Say: **Philippians 4:13 says, "I can do all things through Christ, because he gives me strength." Let's repeat that verse together.** Repeat the verse with the kids, then continue: **We have the strength of Jesus to help us fight the pressure to do things that are wrong. We also have the strength of our Christian friends in this class. Let's lock elbows again, only this time we're going to pull together instead of pulling apart.**

Have kids form a large circle, facing inward. Then have them reach out, lock elbows, and pull each other into a close circle as they each pull their arms to their chests. Say: **Now let's take turns repeating Philippians 4:13. This time we'll fill in each person's name as we say the verse together. We'll start with the person on my left and say, "**(Name of person on your left)**, you can do all things through Christ, because he gives you strength."**

the POINT

Continue around the circle, then close by praying: **Dear God, we've learned that** **real friends don't ask each other to do things that are wrong. Help us to choose friends who will encourage us to follow Jesus. Amen.**

ESCAPE HATCH

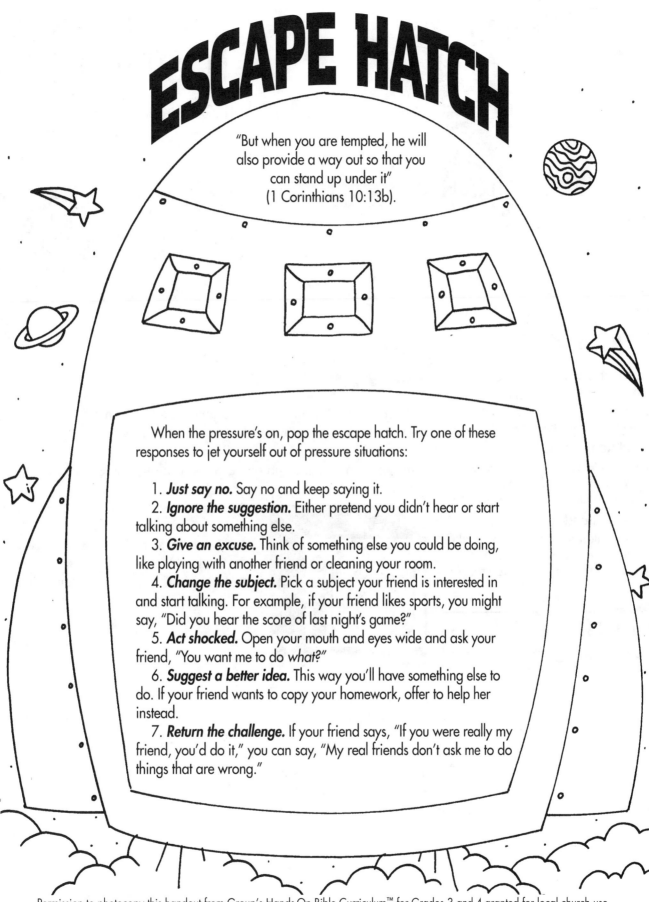

"But when you are tempted, he will also provide a way out so that you can stand up under it" (1 Corinthians 10:13b).

When the pressure's on, pop the escape hatch. Try one of these responses to jet yourself out of pressure situations:

1. *Just say no.* Say no and keep saying it.
2. *Ignore the suggestion.* Either pretend you didn't hear or start talking about something else.
3. *Give an excuse.* Think of something else you could be doing, like playing with another friend or cleaning your room.
4. *Change the subject.* Pick a subject your friend is interested in and start talking. For example, if your friend likes sports, you might say, "Did you hear the score of last night's game?"
5. *Act shocked.* Open your mouth and eyes wide and ask your friend, "You want me to do *what?*"
6. *Suggest a better idea.* This way you'll have something else to do. If your friend wants to copy your homework, offer to help her instead.
7. *Return the challenge.* If your friend says, "If you were really my friend, you'd do it," you can say, "My real friends don't ask me to do things that are wrong."

Hands-On FUN AT HOME

the POINT ☞ **Real friends don't ask you to do things that are wrong.**

■ ■ ■ ■ ■ ■ ■ ■ ■ ■ ■ ■ ■ ■ ■

BIBLE FOCUS

"My command is this: Love each other as I have loved you" (John 15:12).

CHECK it OUT

Read 1 John 1:9.
What's the best thing to do if you let a friend convince you to do something wrong?

Read Romans 5:6-8.
How could you use this verse to tell a friend why you don't want to do anything that would displease God?

Read 2 Timothy 1:7.
How could this verse help you take a stand for what's right when others want you to do something wrong?

ARTicles

FAITH walk

As you watch TV this week, take notes in a special notebook. Write the name of each show you watch. Decide whether what you saw on the show would encourage you to follow God or tempt you to break God's commandments. At the end of the week, talk over these questions with a parent:

● Is this a good show for me to watch? Why or why not?
● If I didn't watch this show, how could I spend my time?
● How much does TV influence how I think and talk?

Use these heart pockets to encourage friends and family to do what's right. You'll need envelopes, scissors, and markers or rubber stamps. Draw two hearts on an envelope as shown, so the bottom point of each heart is a bottom corner of the envelope. Cut out each heart, then decorate one side and write the person's name on it. On the other side, write an encouraging message such as "I like the way you build people up," or "I noticed you were patient with Amy—good job!" Drop a wrapped candy inside the pocket for a doubly sweet message, then deliver your heartfelt encouragement.

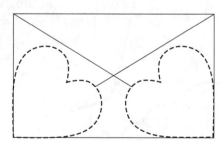

LESSON 13

ALL-WEATHER FRIENDS

"My command is this: Love each other as I have loved you"
(John 15:12).

THE POINT

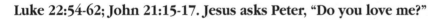

☞ **Real friends still love you, even if you disappoint them.**

THE BIBLE BASIS

Luke 22:54-62; John 21:15-17. Jesus asks Peter, "Do you love me?"

These two passages give us insights into the friendship between Jesus and Peter. Luke tells the sad story of how Peter disappointed Jesus by denying him three times. John tells about another encounter between Jesus and Peter that took place after Jesus had risen from the dead. After asking Peter to renew his love three times, Jesus committed to Peter the task of caring for his earthly flock of new believers.

Third- and fourth-graders can easily identify with Peter. Kids as young as 8 and 9 are under increasing pressure to succeed. They want to please their parents, teachers, and especially their friends. Because third- and fourth-graders value one another's approval so highly, they're bound to let each other down. This lesson will remind kids that everybody makes mistakes. And it will teach them that real friends won't hold mistakes against them forever. By the end of the lesson, kids will learn that real friends, including Jesus, understand and forgive friends who disappoint them.

Other Scriptures used in this lesson are **Matthew 18:21-22** and **Ephesians 4:32.**

GETTING THE POINT

Students will
- hear how Jesus forgave a friend who disappointed him,
- understand that everyone makes mistakes,
- identify ways they can restore broken friendships, and
- affirm friendship qualities they see in each other.

THIS LESSON AT A GLANCE

Before the lesson, collect the necessary items from the Learning Lab for the activities you plan to use. Refer to the pictures in the margin to see what each item looks like.

SECTION	MINUTES	WHAT STUDENTS WILL DO	LEARNING LAB SUPPLIES	CLASSROOM SUPPLIES
ATTENTION GRABBER	up to 10	**CORN CROSSING**—Try to carry corn on stacking clowns without dropping it.	Indian corn, stacking clowns	Paper cups, snack
BIBLE EXPLORATION AND APPLICATION	up to 15	**FROM BAD TO WORSE**—Hear about Peter's denial in Luke 22:54-62 and talk about times they've let others down.	Cassette: "Failure and Forgiveness, Part 1"	Cassette player
	up to 10	**NOBODY'S PERFECT**—Try to perform a series of impossible actions and discover that nobody's perfect, then read Matthew 18:21-22.		Bibles
	up to 15	**PETER, PART 2**—Hear about Peter's restored relationship with Jesus from John 21:15-17 and commit to restoring broken friendships in their lives.	Cassette: "Failure and Forgiveness, Part 2," Indian corn	Bibles, cassette player
CLOSING	up to 10	**FRIENDSHIP CHEFS**—Create a recipe for friendship and affirm friendship qualities in one another.	Chef's hat	Markers or crayons

Remember to make photocopies of the "Hands-On Fun at Home" handout (p. 154) to send home with your kids. The "Fun at Home" handout suggests ways for kids to talk with their families about what they're learning in class and helps them put their faith into action.

THE LESSON

As kids arrive, ask them which "Fun at Home" activities they tried. Ask questions such as "Which TV shows encouraged you to follow God?" and "How did you encourage someone last week?"

Tell kids that whenever you ring the *gold foil bell,* they are to stop talking, raise their hands, and focus on you. Explain that it's important to respond to this signal quickly so the class can do as many fun activities as possible.

ATTENTION GRABBER

CORN CROSSING
(up to 10 minutes)

LEARNING LAB

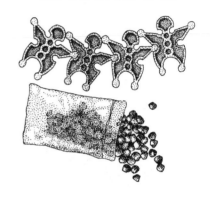

Today our lesson is about forgiveness, and this activity will give everyone a chance to practice forgiveness. We'll be racing to carry corn across the room.

Have kids line up in two teams. Divide the *Indian corn* between two paper cups and give each team a cup of corn and a *stacking clown.* Put an empty cup for each team on the other side of the room.

Say: **The object of this race is to transport all your *Indian corn* to the cup on the other side of the room. Use your *stacking clown* to scoop out and carry the corn as you hop across the room. If you drop any corn, you must pick it up and start over. When you get all your corn into the cup, give the clown scoop to the next person. If both teams can fill their cups within two minutes, we'll have a snack.**

After two minutes, ring the *gold foil bell.* Wait for kids to respond, then check to see if teams have filled their cups. Place the cups and the *stacking clowns* out of sight. Say: **Well, that was a hard race! It looks like both teams made mistakes by dropping lots of corn.**

But both teams did a great job anyway, and I'm not going to hold back your snack just because you made a few mistakes. Before I get the snacks, though, let's show we've forgiven one another's mistakes by giving each other high five's for doing such a great job.

As kids enjoy their snacks, discuss the following questions.

● **How did you feel when kids on your team kept dropping the corn?** (Upset; disappointed; frustrated.)

● **How do you feel now that you've forgiven one another for your mistakes?** (Sorry I was mad; silly; glad we got snacks anyway.)

Say: **When you saw everyone dropping the corn during the race, you were all pretty disappointed. Today we're going to hear about a friend who disappointed Jesus. Even though Jesus was very disappointed, he still forgave his friend.**  **Real friends still love you, even if you disappoint them.**

TEACHER TIP

It's important to say The Point just as it's written in each activity. Repeating The Point over and over will help kids remember it and apply it to their lives.

✎ the POINT

LEARNING LAB

FROM BAD TO WORSE
(up to 15 minutes)

Say: **Things were looking pretty bad for Jesus and his friends. Jesus had just been arrested, and his friends wondered if everything they had hoped for was about to end. And then things went from bad to worse.**

Play "Failure and Forgiveness, Part 1" on the *cassette tape*.

After the cassette segment, have kids form pairs and discuss the following questions. Pause after you ask each question to allow time for discussion. Ask:

● **How do you think Peter felt when he said he didn't know his friend Jesus?** (Afraid; angry; sad.)

● **When have you felt like Peter?** (When I told a lie; when I didn't do my homework; when I called my brother a name.)

● **What do you do when you know you've done something to hurt or disappoint a friend?** (Say, "I'm sorry"; ask for forgiveness; cry.)

● **What can you do when you know you've done something that would disappoint Jesus?** (Pray; ask for forgiveness; say I'm sorry.)

After kids have finished discussing the last question, ring the *gold foil bell*. Wait for kids to respond. Have volunteers report their discoveries to the rest of the class. Then say: **We've all had times when we've disappointed the people we care about.**  **But real friends still love you, even if you disappoint them. Real friends give us chances to try again.**

the POINT

NOBODY'S PERFECT
(up to 10 minutes)

Say: **Now I'd like you to stand up and scatter around the room. Try to stand at least an arm's length away from the people near you.**

I'm going to give you a few simple instructions. All you need to do is follow them. Each time I read an action, add that action to the other actions you're doing. If you can't do all of the actions, you must sit down.

Read the following list of instructions. Allow time for kids to add each new activity before reading the next one.

● **Raise your right foot.**
● **Snap your fingers on one hand.**
● **Clap the hand of a partner with your other hand.**
● **Hop up and down.**
● **Shake your head.**

TEACHER TIP

If you have a small classroom, take your class outside or to another area of the church for this activity. Make sure to choose an area where you won't disturb another class.

- Sing "Mary Had a Little Lamb."
- Spin around.
- Raise your left foot.

After you give the last instruction, kids will probably protest that you've asked them to do the impossible. At this point, have them all sit down. Ask:

- **What was it like to do all those actions at once?** (Fun; easy until I had to raise my left foot; tiring.)
- **Why couldn't you raise your left foot?** (Because I was doing too many other things; because I didn't want to fall down.)
- **How is this activity like real life?** (Sometimes you can't do everything at once; sometimes people ask you to do things that are impossible.)
- **In this activity you had to sit down if you couldn't follow the instructions; what happens in real life when you can't do everything you're supposed to do?** (I have to give something up; people get mad at me if I forget to do something.)

Say: **When we can't do everything we're supposed to do, we may let somebody down. Peter thought he could stay with Jesus until the very end, but that was too hard for him. Jesus may have been disappointed that his friend Peter had let him down, but he forgave Peter anyway. Even though we don't mean to, sooner or later we're bound to disappoint someone, just as Peter disappointed Jesus. We can either let that disappointment spoil our friendship, or we can ask our friend's forgiveness. Let's read what Jesus taught Peter about forgiveness.**

Form pairs, then distribute Bibles and have kids read **Matthew 18:21-22** with their partners. After pairs have had time to read the passage, have them discuss the following questions:

- **Is it easy or hard to forgive someone? Explain.** (Hard, because sometimes I'd rather just stay mad; easy if the person is really sorry.)
- **What are your feelings after you've forgiven someone?** (Good; glad we're still friends.)
- **What is it like to be forgiven?** (I'm relieved; I feel like I have a fresh start.)

After several minutes, ring the *gold foil bell*. Wait for kids to respond, then invite them to share their responses with the rest of the class. Say: **Sometimes it's easier to forgive others if we remember how it feels to be forgiven. Nobody's perfect, and if we remember all the times we've let our friends down, it's easier to forgive them when they disappoint us. If you let a friend down, you should ask that person to forgive you. And if a friend lets you down, you should forgive that person—over and over again if you have to.** ☞ **Real friends still love you, even if you disappoint them.**

 the POINT

LEARNING LAB

BIBLE INSIGHT

In Greek, the two terms from John 21:15-17 that are translated into the word "love" are "agapaō" and "phileō." Jesus used "agapaō" in his first two questions to Peter. This word implies divine love and is the same word used in John 3:16. "Phileō," used in Jesus' third question to Peter, implies affinity or fondness. The words here were used interchangeably to imply the bond of love between God and men.

the POINT 👉

PETER, PART 2
(up to 15 minutes)

Say: **Let's rejoin the story of Jesus and Peter. A few minutes ago, we heard how Peter denied his friend Jesus. Listen to what happened the next time Peter and Jesus talked.**

Play "Failure and Forgiveness, Part 2" from the *cassette tape.*

After the cassette segment, ask:

● **Why do you think Jesus asked Peter if he loved him?** (Because Peter denied him; he wanted to make sure he could trust Peter.)

Say: **Other parts of the Bible tell us that Jesus takes care of his followers like a shepherd takes care of sheep. When Jesus said, "Feed my sheep," he was asking Peter to take care of his friends on earth after he went up to heaven.** Ask:

● **What are some ways we can take care of our friends today?** (Let your friends know you care about them; try to help when a friend feels sad or upset.)

Say: **Forgiving our friends is one way to show we love them. Let's read about that now.** Have kids look up **Ephesians 4:32.** When everyone has found the verse, ask a volunteer to read it aloud. Then say: **Think of a friend or family member you've disappointed recently. You don't need to say the person's name out loud. Maybe you promised to help your friend build a treehouse, and you forgot; maybe you stayed late at a friend's house and didn't help your mom or dad with the chores. Raise your hand when you have that person in mind.**

As kids raise their hands, give them each one or two kernels of *Indian corn,* then continue: **Take your *Indian corn* home and put it in a wet paper towel. Set it in a sunny place and keep the paper towel moist until the corn seed sprouts. Then plant the seed in a pot. As you take care of the seed you've planted, remember that friendships need care too.** 👉 **Real friends still love you, even if you disappoint them. So when we disappoint our friends, we need to ask them to forgive us. And when friends disappoint us or let us down, we should forgive them just as Jesus forgave Peter. By planting seeds of forgiveness, we can encourage our friendships to grow.**

Hands-On FUN AT HOME

We believe that Christian education extends beyond the classroom into the home. Photocopy the "Hands-On Fun at Home" handout (p. 154) for this week and send it home with your kids. Encourage kids to try several activities and discuss the Bible verses and questions with their parents.

CLOSING

FRIENDSHIP CHEFS
(up to 10 minutes)

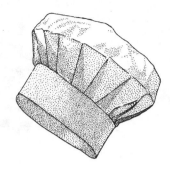

Before class, write two of the following lesson Points on each side of the band of the *chef's hat*:

- Real friends stick up for each other.
- Real friends comfort each other when they're sad.
- Real friends don't ask you to do things that are wrong.
- Real friends still love you, even if you disappoint them.

Read each of The Points and ask kids how they've been able to apply them to their lives.

Say: **For the last four weeks, we've been learning how to be real friends. Let's use that knowledge now. If we were making a recipe for friendship, what ingredients would we need? Think of your favorite friendship ingredient, such as love, kindness, or loyalty, then write it on the *chef's hat*.**

Distribute markers or crayons and let kids take turns writing on the *chef's hat*. When kids have written their friendship ingredients, have them stand in a circle. Say: **I hope we've all become real friends because of what we've learned. We're going to take a few minutes now to appreciate the friends we have in our class. We'll each take a turn holding the hat. I'll give the hat to the person on my right, first. Then I'll pick one of the friendship ingredients we've listed on the hat and say, "**(Name of person)**, you're a real friend because you're loyal." Then** (name of person) **can give the hat to the next person. After you've held the hat, sit down.**

After all the kids are seated, hang the *chef's hat* in your classroom. Close with a prayer similar to this one: **Dear God, thank you for all our friends in this class. Help us follow Jesus' example and practice the friendship qualities we've learned. Make us real friends and help us to forgive others as you've forgiven us. Thank you for showing us that**  **real friends still love us, even when we disappoint them. In Jesus' name, amen.**

TEACHER TIP

If you have a large class or you're running short on time, simply have kids pass the hat around and repeat together, "(Name of student), you're a real friend."

✍ the POINT

Hands-On FUN! AT HOME

LESSON 13:
ALL-WEATHER FRIENDS

the POINT ☞ **Real friends still love you, even if you disappoint them.**

"My command is this: Love each other as I have loved you" (John 15:12).

BIBLE FOCUS

FAITH walk

Read John 21:15-17 with your family. Talk about ways you can care for each other, then set up a "Sheep Shop" in a corner of your living or family room. Glue cotton balls to index cards and write on each card ways to care for different members of the family. You might care for a younger brother or sister by reading a story. You might care for your mom or dad by keeping the kitchen clean for a day. Assign a different member of your family to be the shepherd each day. Have family members check in with the shepherd to receive cards with their caring assignments for that day.

CHECK it OUT

Read Colossians 3:13-14.
How can loving someone help you forgive them?

Read Luke 15:11-32.
What's the hardest thing you've ever had to forgive someone for?

FORGIVENESS feast

Set aside one night this week to share a Family Forgiveness Feast. Have everyone in your family pitch in to make I'm Sorry Salad, I Forgive You French Fries, Forgiveness Fish Sticks, and Prayer Pie.

Before you enjoy your meal together, read John 15:12 to your family and let each person thank the others for their love and forgiveness.

WAY to PRAY

Pray the Lord's Prayer together from Matthew 6:9-13. After you've recited verse 12, pause for a moment to allow family members to pray silently for those they need to forgive. Then finish the prayer and ask God to help you forgive others.

BONUS IDEAS

■ ■ ■ ■ ■ ■ ■ ■ ■ ■ ■ ■ ■

GREAT GAMES

Tree-Decorating Contest—Form three teams. Give each team a *pine cone* and an assortment of craft supplies. Tell kids they'll have five minutes to create wonderful Christmas trees out of their *pine cones.* Explain that you'll be giving awards to the best trees in the following categories: funniest, most creative, and most beautiful. You might even want to invite independent judges to determine the awards. Give an award for each tree, and if a tree doesn't fit your original categories, invent another title to fit it. This activity works well with the lessons on Jesus' birth.

Three-Handed Wrap—Form pairs and give each pair a *metallic ribbon,* a *neon loop,* and a rolled-up sheet of paper. Have partners stand side by side, hold hands, and bind their hands together with the *neon loops.* Explain that when you say "go," the pairs should pick up the *metallic ribbons* and tie them in a bow around their sheets of paper without removing their hands from the *neon loops.* The first pair to tie its sheet of paper successfully wins. This activity works well with the lessons on friendship.

Friendship Relay—Set up three or four stations in a large room or outside your church. Post a sign at each station listing a task that must be performed. Include tasks such as blowing up balloons, switching shoes, jumping rope, or carrying another person piggyback. Form two teams and have each team member choose a partner. Both partners must complete each task before they can move on to the next station. As partners finish a station, the team may send out another pair. The team whose partners finish all the stations in the shortest amount of time wins the game. This game works well with the lessons on friendship.

Nature's Miracles Scavenger Hunt—Send kids on a scavenger hunt to discover God's miracles in nature. Form teams of no more than four and give them no more than 10 minutes to search for the items listed below. Make sure you clearly define safe boundaries and restrictions. You may need to adapt the list to suit the climate and physical features of the grounds around your church.

    a rock or pebble—1 point
    a blade of grass—1 point
    a caterpillar—10 points
    a snail—5 points
    any other live insect—4 points
    a spider web—3 points
    a piece of tree bark—1 point
    a dandelion—3 points
    any other flower—2 points
    a pine cone—2 points
    other natural miracles—award points at your discretion

Designate a return meeting point outdoors where you'll evaluate teams' findings and total the points. The team with the most points wins. If you decide to give prizes, consider giving prizes to the team with the most unusual item and the team that finished fastest as well as the team with the most points. This activity works well with the lessons on miracles.

AFFIRMATION ACTIVITIES

Stocking Stuffers—Have kids make stockings by cutting out two paper stocking shapes and stapling the side and bottom edges together. Let kids decorate their stockings and remind them to write their names somewhere on the outside. Hang the stockings on a wall or bulletin board. Distribute strips of paper and pencils and have everyone write an affirmation stocking stuffer for each person in the group. If kids need ideas, suggest that they name something they admire about each person. Have kids drop their affirmations in each other's stockings. When all the stockings are stuffed, say, "Merry Christmas!" and let kids read their messages.

Praise Your Pals, Pass the *Pine Cone*—Use the *pine cone* from the Learning Lab for this Hot-Potato-style game. Have kids pass the *pine cone* around the circle as you play music. When the music stops, kids left holding the *pine cone* may stay in the game if, within 10 seconds, they can think of a reason the person on their right would be a good friend. Play the game until everyone has been affirmed, or longer if kids enjoy it. For even more fun, add a second *pine cone.*

Blown Away—Set the *multicolored feathers* in a pile on the floor. Several feet away from the pile of feathers, tape a 2-foot masking tape square. Give one student two feathers and have him or her stand inside the taped square. Give the rest of the kids 15 seconds to blow as many feathers into the square as they can. After 15 seconds, ring the *gold foil bell.* Wait for kids to respond, then count the feathers inside the square. For each one, have kids think of one reason they appreciate the student in the square. Don't forget to include the two feathers you gave the student at the beginning. Repeat the activity until all the kids have been affirmed.

PARTIES AND PROJECTS

A Festival of Gifts—Ask several adults who enjoy craft projects to staff a Saturday morning gift festival. Have your volunteers plan three or four Christmas gifts (such as ornaments, paperweights, or potholders) kids could make for their parents and teach kids how to make them. Let kids choose one or two gift projects they'd like to complete. After everyone has completed one project, take a doughnut-and-juice break. Adults and kids will get to know one another better, and parents will be pleased that their kids are learning to give.

The Next Best Thing to Swaddling Clothes—Christmas is a wonderful time to remember babies in need. Have the kids in your class organize and carry out a "diaper drive" in your congregation and/or community. Diapers are a huge expense for poor families and emergency shelters that provide temporary lodging for mothers with babies. Establish a time and place for people to bring diapers, then have kids make posters and announcements for the collection. After the collection date, plan a time for your group to help distribute the diapers.

Christmas Around the World—Adopt one of these ideas for your kids to perform during their class or church Christmas party this year:

In Italy, people eat little or no food on the day before Christmas. That night, the family gathers around a miniature scene of Bethlehem containing small figures of Mary and Joseph, the shepherds, and the wise men. As the family prays, the mother puts the bambino (infant Jesus) in the manger. Then Christmas gifts are given.

In Poland, people go without food the whole day before Christmas, then have a feast on Christmas Eve. Families put a vacant chair at their table for Jesus. They scatter a few straws on the table as a reminder of the stable where Christ was born.

Mexican families celebrate *La Posada* on the nine nights before Christmas Day. Family members act out Mary and Joseph's search for a place to stay on the first Christmas Eve. The family proceeds from room to room, led by two children who carry figures of Mary and Joseph. The children beg to enter at the door of each room but are refused. When they reach the room with a miniature stable scene, they are admitted. They put the figures of Mary and Joseph by the manger, but they don't put Jesus in the manger until Christmas Eve.

Friendship Costume Party—Host a costume party at the church or in someone's home. Before the party, assign costume partners and have kids come dressed in costumes that require two people. Costume partners could wear costumes that complement each other, such as Batman and Robin; or one costume that requires two people, such as a horse or other four-legged animal. Encourage creativity; costumes don't have to be fancy to be fun.

Friendship Service Day—Have kids work together in pairs to do various service projects for people in the church. Let your congregation know that the kids in your class want to help them. Possible tasks could include yardwork, washing cars, or sorting classroom supplies. Kids will have fun working with their friends, and church members will enjoy getting to know the kids who volunteer. This activity works well with the lessons on friendship.

Make Some New Friends—Arrange for your class to visit an orphanage or children's home for a day of recreation. If the weather's warm, have the kids play outside. Take along a picnic and play games such as Frisbee, softball, or tag. If the weather's cold or rainy, enjoy an afternoon of indoor games. This activity gives your class a chance to make new friends.

Tell us what you think

Please help Group Publishing continue to provide innovative and exciting resources to help your children know, love, and follow Christ. Take a moment to fill out and send back this survey. Thanks!

1. What level(s) and what quarter(s) of Hands-On Bible Curriculum™ are you using?

2. How many children are in your class? adult helpers?

3. How has the size of your class changed since using Hands-On Bible Curriculum?

❏ Remained the same   ❏ Grown a lot
❏ Grown a little   ❏ Other _____

Comments

4. When do you use Hands-On Bible Curriculum?

❏ Sunday school   ❏ Midweek group
❏ Children's church   ❏ Other (please describe) _____
                                         _____
                                         _____

5. What do you like best about the curriculum?

6. Is there anything about the curriculum you would like to see changed? (For example, if a certain lesson didn't work well, what specific changes would you recommend?)

7. What products would you like to see Group Publishing develop to fill specific needs in your church?

Name_____

Church Name _____

Denomination _____ Church Size _____

Church Address _____

City _____ State _____ ZIP _____

Church Phone _____

E-mail _____

TEACH YOUR PRESCHOOLERS AS JESUS TAUGHT WITH GROUP'S *HANDS-ON BIBLE CURRICULUM*™

Hands-On Bible Curriculum™ **for preschoolers** helps your preschoolers learn the way they learn best—by touching, exploring, and discovering. With active learning, preschoolers love learning about the Bible, and they really remember what they learn.

Because small children learn best through repetition, Preschoolers and Pre-K & K will learn one important point per lesson, and Toddlers & 2s will learn one point each month with **Hands-On Bible Curriculum**. These important lessons will stick with them and comfort them during their daily lives. Your children will learn:

- •God is our friend,
- •who Jesus is, and
- •we can always trust Jesus.

The **Learning Lab**® is packed with age-appropriate learning tools for fun, faith-building lessons. Toddlers & 2s explore big **Interactive StoryBoards**™ with enticing textures that toddlers love to touch—like sandpaper for earth, cotton for clouds, and blue cellophane for water. While they hear the Bible story, children also *touch* the Bible story. And they learn. **Bible Big Books**™ captivate Preschoolers and Pre-K & K while teaching them important Bible lessons. With **Jumbo Bible Puzzles**™ and involving **Learning Mats**™, your children will see, touch, and explore their Bible stories. Each quarter there's a brand new collection of supplies to keep your lessons fresh and involving.

Fuzzy, age-appropriate hand puppets are also available to add to the learning experience. What better way to teach your class than with the help of an attention-getting teaching assistant? These child-friendly puppets help you teach each lesson with scripts provided in the **Teachers Guide**. Plus, your children will enjoy teaching the puppets what they learn. Cuddles the Lamb, Whiskers the Mouse, and Pockets the Kangaroo turn each lesson into an interactive and entertaining learning experience.

Just order one **Learning Lab** and one **Teachers Guide** for each age level, add a few common classroom supplies, and presto—you have everything you need to inspire and build faith in your children. For more interactive fun, introduce your children to the age-appropriate puppet who will be your teaching assistant and their friend. No student books are required!

Hands-On Bible Curriculum is also available for elementary grades.

Order today from your local Christian bookstore, or write: Group Publishing, P.O. Box 485, Loveland, CO 80539.